TSI

Math Workbook

Abundant Exercises and Two Full-Length TSI Math Practice Tests

By
Michael Smith & Reza Nazari

TSI Math Workbook

Published in the United State of America By

The Math Notion

Email: info@Mathnotion.com

Web: www.MathNotion.com

Copyright © 2019 by the Math Notion. All rights reserved. No part of this publication may be reproduced, stored in a retrieval system, or transmitted in any form or by any means, electronic, mechanical, photocopying, recording, scanning, or otherwise, except as permitted under Section 107 or 108 of the 1976 United States Copyright Ac, without permission of the author.

All inquiries should be addressed to the Math Notion.

TSI Math Workbook

TSI Math Workbook covers all Math topics you will ever need to prepare for the TSI Math test. This workbook contains the key areas of the TSI Math. It reviews the most important components of the TSI test. This workbook offers plenty of practice questions to challenge students for achieving the high score on their real TSI Math test. TSI Math Workbook is the ideal prep solution for anyone who wants to pass the TSI Math test. Not only does it provide abundant math exercises, but it also contains practice test questions as well as detailed explanations of each answer.

This Math workbook is filled with exercises and worksheets covering fundamental math, arithmetic, algebra, geometry, basic statistics, probability, and data analysis. Answers are provided for all math questions, and two full-length TSI Math tests with detailed answers and explanations can help you discover your weak areas for concentrated study. Here is comprehensive preparation for the TSI Math section, and a valuable learning tool for the TSI test takers who need to improve their knowledge of Mathematics and prepare for the TSI Math test.

Each chapter and topic of the book go into detail to cover all the content likely to appear on the TSI test. This completely revised edition reflects all the new types of math questions that will appear on the TSI.

Developed by experienced TSI Math teachers and authors for test takers trying to achieve a passing score on the TSI test, this comprehensive Math workbook includes:

- Over 2,000 revised Math questions to practice with
- Easy–to–follow activities
- Fun and interactive exercises that build confidence
- Topics are grouped by category, so you can easily focus on the topics you struggle on
- 2 Full-length and REAL TSI Math tests
- Detailed answers and explanations for the TSI Math practice tests

After completing this workbook, you will gain confidence, strong foundation, and adequate practice to ace the TSI Math test.

Get the help and confidence you need to be well prepared for the TSI Math test!

About the Author

Michael Smith has been a math instructor for over a decade now. He holds a master's degree in Management. Since 2006, Michael has devoted his time to both teaching and developing exceptional math learning materials. As a Math instructor and test prep expert, Michael has worked with thousands of students. He has used the feedback of his students to develop a unique study program that can be used by students to drastically improve their math score fast and effectively.

– GRE Math Workbook

– ACCUPLACER Math Workbook

– SAT Math Workbook

– PSAT Math Workbook

– ACT Math Workbook

– GED Math Workbook

– HiSET Math Workbook

– and many Math Education Workbooks…

As an experienced Math teacher, Mr. Smith employs a variety of formats to help students achieve their goals: He tutors online and in person, he teaches students in large groups, and he provides training materials and textbooks through his website and through Amazon.

You can contact Michael via email at:

info@Mathnotion.com

WWW.MathNotion.COM

... So Much More Online!

✓ FREE Math lessons

✓ More Math learning books!

✓ Mathematics Worksheets

✓ Online Math Tutors

Need a PDF version of this book?

Please visit www.MathNotion.com

TSI Math Workbook

Contents

Chapter 1: Integer and Complex Numbers 15
    Adding and Subtracting Integers 16
    Multiplying and Dividing Integers 17
    Arrange, Order, and Comparing Integers 18
    Order of Operations 19
    Integers and Absolute Value 20
    Adding and Subtracting Complex Numbers 21
    Multiplying and Dividing Complex Numbers 22
    Graphing Complex Numbers 23
    Rationalizing Imaginary Denominators 24
    Answers of Worksheets – Chapter 1 25

Chapter 2: Fractions and Decimals 29
    Factoring Numbers 30
    Greatest Common Factor (GCF) 31
    Least Common Multiple (LCM) 31
    Divisibility Rules 32
    Simplifying Fractions 33
    Adding and Subtracting Fractions 34
    Multiplying and Dividing Fractions 35
    Adding and Subtracting Mixed Numbers 36
    Multiplying and Dividing Mixed Numbers 37
    Comparing Decimals 38
    Rounding Decimals 39
    Adding and Subtracting Decimals 40
    Multiplying and Dividing Decimals 41
    Converting Between Fractions, Decimals and Mixed Numbers 42

TSI Math Workbook

Answers of Worksheets – Chapter 2 43
Chapter 3: Proportion, Ratio, Percent 49
    Writing and Simplifying Ratios 50
    Create a Proportion 51
    Similar Figures 51
    Ratio and Rates Word Problems 52
    Percentage Calculations 53
    Percent Problems 54
    Markup, Discount, and Tax 54
    Simple Interest 55
    Converting Between Percent, Fractions, and Decimals 56
    Answers of Worksheets – Chapter 3 57
Chapter 4: Sequences and Series 59
    Arithmetic Sequences 60
    Geometric Sequences 61
    Comparing Arithmetic and Geometric Sequences 62
    Finite Geometric Series 63
    Infinite Geometric Series 64
    Answers of Worksheets – Chapter 4 65
Chapter 5: Exponents and Radicals 67
    Multiplication Property of Exponents 68
    Division Property of Exponents 68
    Powers of Products and Quotients 69
    Zero and Negative Exponents 70
    Negative Exponents and Negative Bases 70
    Writing Scientific Notation 71
    Square Roots 71
    Simplifying Radical Expressions 72
    Simplifying Radical Expressions Involving Fractions 73
    Multiplying Radical Expressions 74

TSI Math Workbook

Adding and Subtracting Radical Expressions 75

Solving Radical Equations 76

Domain and Range of Radical Functions.. 77

Answers of Worksheets – Chapter 5... 78

Chapter 6: Logarithms.. 82

Rewriting Logarithms 83

Evaluating Logarithms 83

Properties of Logarithms 84

Natural Logarithms 84

Solving Exponential Equations Requiring Logarithms.. 85

Solving Logarithmic Equations 86

Answers of Worksheets – Chapter 6... 87

Chapter 7: Linear Functions 89

Relation and Functions 90

Slope and Rate of Change 91

xandy intercepts 93

Slope–intercept Form 94

Point–slope Form 95

Equation of Parallel or Perpendicular Lines.. 96

Graphing Lines of Equations 97

Equations of Horizontal and Vertical Lines 98

Function Notation 99

Adding and Subtracting Functions 100

Multiplying and Dividing Functions... 101

Composition of Functions 102

Answers of Worksheets – Chapter 7... 103

Chapter 8 Equations and Inequalities 109

One–Step Equations... 110

Two–Step Equations 111

Multi–Step Equations... 112

Graphing Single–Variable Inequalities 113
One–Step Inequalities 114
Two–Step Inequalities 115
Multi–Step Inequalities 115
Solving Systems of Equations by Substitution 116
Solving Systems of Equations by Elimination 117
Systems of Equations Word Problems 118
Graphing Linear Inequalities 119
Finding Distance of Two Points 120
Answers of Worksheets – Chapter 8 121

Chapter 9: Polynomials 127
Classifying Polynomials 128
Simplifying Polynomials 129
Adding and Subtracting Polynomials 130
Multiplying Monomials 130
Multiply Binomials 131
Multiply and Divide Monomials 131
Multiply a Polynomial and a Monomial 132
Factor Trinomials 132
Operations with Polynomials 133
Answers of Worksheets – Chapter 9 134

Chapter 10: Quadratic Functions 137
Graphing Quadratic Functions 138
Solving Quadratic Equations 139
Use the Quadratic Formula and the Discriminant 140
Solve Quadratic Inequalities 141
Adding and Subtracting Matrices 142
Matrix Multiplication .... **Error! Bookmark not defined.**
Finding Determinants of a Matrix 143
Finding Inverse of a Matrix 145

Matrix Equations 146
Answers of Worksheets – Chapter 10 147

Chapter 11: Trigonometric Functions 151

Trig ratios of General Angles 152
Sketch Each Angle in Standard Position 153
Finding Co-terminal Angles and Reference Angles 154
Writing Each Measure in Radians 155
Writing Each Measure in Degrees 156
Evaluating Each Trigonometric Function 157
Missing Sides and Angles of a Right Triangle 158
Arc Length and Sector Area 159
Answers of Worksheets – Chapter 11 160

Chapter 12: Geometry - Plane and solid Figures 163

Transformations: Translations, Rotations, and Reflections 164
The Pythagorean Theorem 165
Area of Triangles 166
Area of Trapezoids 167
Area and Perimeter of Quadrilateral 168
Area and Circumference of Circles 170
Volume of Cubes 171
Volume of Rectangle Prisms 172
Surface Area of Cubes 173
Surface Area of a Rectangle Prism 174
Volume of a Cylinder 175
Surface Area of a Cylinder 176
Volume of Pyramids and Cones 177
Surface Area of Pyramids and Cones 178
Answers of Worksheets – Chapter 12 179

Chapter 13: Statistics and Probability 183

Mean and Median 184

TSI Math Workbook

- Mode and Range 185
- Histograms 186
- Box and Whisker Plot 187
- Bar Graph 187
- Dot plots 188
- Scatter Plots 189
- Stem–And–Leaf Plot 190
- The Pie Graph or Circle Graph 191
- Probability of Simple Events 192
- Experimental Probability 193
- Factorials 194
- Permutations 195
- Combination 196
- Answers of Worksheets – Chapter 13 197

TSI Math Test Review 201
- TSI Math Practice Test Answer Sheets 203
- TSI Math Practice Test 1 205
- TSI Math Practice Test 2 213

Answers and Explanations 221
- Answer Key 221
- Practice Tests 1 223
- Practice Tests 2 227

Chapter 1:

Integer and Complex Numbers

Topics that you'll learn in this chapter:

- Rounding and Estimates
- Addition and Subtraction Integers
- Multiplication and Division Integers
- Arrange and ordering Integers and Numbers
- Comparing Integers, Order of Operations
- Mixed Integer Computations
- Integers and Absolute Value
- Adding and Subtracting Complex Numbers
- Multiplying and Dividing Complex Numbers
- Graphing Complex Numbers
- Rationalizing Imaginary Denominators

"Wherever there is number, there is beauty." –Proclus

Adding and Subtracting Integers

✎ **Find the sum.**

1) $(-14) + (-5)$

2) $7 + (-21)$

3) $(-15) + 24$

4) $(-9) + 28$

5) $33 + (-14)$

6) $(-23) + (-4) + 3$

7) $3 + (-16) + (-20) + (-19)$

8) $(-28) + (-19) + 31 + 16$

9) $(-7) + (-11) + (27 - 19)$

10) $6 + (-20) + (35 - 24)$

11) $(+24) + (+32) + (-47)$

12) $41 + 17 + (-29)$

✎ **Find the difference.**

13) $(-6) - (-32)$

14) $(-14) - (9)$

15) $(26) - (-8)$

16) $(42) - (7)$

17) $(-13) - (-7) - (19)$

18) $(64) - (-3) + (-6)$

19) $(7) - (4) - (-2)$

20) $(3) - (5) - (-14)$

21) $(24) - (3) - (-24)$

22) $(-37) - (-72)$

23) $(-11) - 24 + 32$

24) $32 - (-16) - (-13)$

Multiplying and Dividing Integers

Find each product.

1) $(-7) \times (-4)$

2) 7×6

3) $(-3) \times 7 \times (-4)$

4) $3 \times (-7) \times (-7)$

5) $12 \times (-14)$

6) $20 \times (-6)$

7) 9×8

8) $(-5) \times (-13)$

9) $7 \times (-8) \times 3$

10) $8 \times (-1) \times 5$

11) $(-7) \times (-9)$

12) $(-12) \times (-11) \times 2$

Find each quotient.

13) $56 \div 8$

14) $(-60) \div 4$

15) $(-72) \div (-8)$

16) $28 \div (-7)$

17) $38 \div (-2)$

18) $(-84) \div (-12)$

19) $37 \div (-1)$

20) $(-169) \div 13$

21) $81 \div 9$

22) $(-24) \div (-3)$

23) $(-6) \div (-1)$

24) $(-65) \div 5$

Arrange, Order, and Comparing Integers

📝 Order each set of integers from least to greatest.

1) −12, −17, 12, −1, 1   ___, ___, ___, ___, ___, ___

2) 11, −7, 5, −3, 2   ___, ___, ___, ___, ___, ___

3) 25, −52, 19, 0, −22   ___, ___, ___, ___, ___, ___

4) 31, −84, 0, −13, 47, −55   ___, ___, ___, ___, ___, ___

5) −45, 39, 21, −18, −51, 42   ___, ___, ___, ___, ___, ___

6) −17, −65, 71, −25, −51, −39   ___, ___, ___, ___, ___, ___

📝 Order each set of integers from greatest to least.

7) 81, 5, 36, 19, 77, 24   ___, ___, ___, ___, ___, ___

8) −1, 7, −3, 4, −7   ___, ___, ___, ___, ___, ___

9) −47, 17, −17, 27, 37   ___, ___, ___, ___, ___, ___

10) −21, 19, −14, −17, 15   ___, ___, ___, ___, ___, ___

11) 1, 0, −1, −2, 2, -3   ___, ___, ___, ___, ___, ___

12) −124, −91, 31, −28, −75, 19   ___, ___, ___, ___, ___, ___

Compare. Use >, =, <

1) 0 ___ 1

2) −12 ___ −17

3) 0 ___ −21

4) 41 ___ −56

5) −654 ___ −645

6) −42 ___ −48

7) −68 ___ −20

8) −86 ___ −106

9) −26 ___ (−26)

10) 425 ___ −425

Order of Operations

Evaluate each expression.

1) $41 - (8 \times 3)$

2) $7 \times 6 - (\dfrac{16}{12 - (-4)})$

3) $32 - (4 \times (-2))$

4) $(6 \times 5) + (-3)$

5) $(\dfrac{(-2)+4}{(-1)+(-1)}) \times (-6)$

6) $(14 + (-2) - 3) \times 7 - 5$

7) $\dfrac{40}{3(9-(-1)) - 10}$

8) $38 - (4 \times 6)$

9) $43 + (4 \times 8)$

10) $((-12) + 18) \div (-2)$

11) $(-60 \div 3) \div (-12 - 8)$

12) $47 + (-8) \times (\dfrac{(-18)}{6})$

Integers and Absolute Value

✎ **Write absolute value of each number.**

1) 22

2) − 12

3) − 31

4) 0

5) 47

6) − 9

7) − 1

8) 37

9) -23

10) − 4

11) − 57

12) 19

13) − 15

14) − 55

✎ **Evaluate.**

15) $|-29| - |13| + 20$

16) $39 + |-15 - 42| - |3|$

17) $28 - |-47| - 61$

18) $|56| - |-18| + 19$

19) $|101| - |-38| - 20$

20) $|42| - |-68| + 70$

21) $|-87 + 73| + 15 - 9$

22) $|-6| + |-17|$

23) $|-9 + 5 - 2| + |6 + 6|$

24) $|-14| - |-23| - 5$

Adding and Subtracting Complex Numbers

Simplify.

1) $-6 + (3i) + (-6 + 5i)$

2) $10 - (6i) + (5 - 12i)$

3) $-3 + (-5 - 6i) - 8$

4) $(-15 - 4i) + (12 + 6i)$

5) $(4 + 2i) + (9 + 3i)$

6) $(6 - 2i) + (3 + i)$

7) $3 + (4 - 4i)$

8) $(9 + 9i) + (6 + 5i)$

9) $(-4i) - (-6 + 2i)$

10) $(-12 + 2i) - (-10 - 10i)$

11) $(-12i) + (2 - 4i) + 8$

12) $(-10 - 8i) - (-8 - 2i)$

13) $(13i) - (15 + 3i)$

14) $(-2 + 4i) - (-6 - i)$

15) $(-3 + 15i) - (-5 + 5i)$

16) $(-12i) + (3 - 4i) + 5$

Multiplying and Dividing Complex Numbers

🖉 Simplify.

1) $(2i)(-i)(2-5i)$

2) $(2-5i)(2-4i)$

3) $(-3+6i)(2+5i)$

4) $(5+3i)(5+8i)$

5) $(2+3i)^2$

6) $3(3i)-(2i)(-5+3i)$

7) $\dfrac{3+2i}{12+2i}$

8) $\dfrac{2-2i}{-3i}$

9) $\dfrac{2+6i}{-1+8i}$

10) $\dfrac{-5+i}{-7+i}$

11) $\dfrac{4+5i}{i}$

12) $\dfrac{-2i}{4-2i}$

13) $\dfrac{2}{-9i}$

14) $\dfrac{-2-6i}{4i}$

15) $\dfrac{9i}{3-i}$

16) $\dfrac{-1+3i}{-6-5i}$

17) $\dfrac{-2-4i}{-2+3i}$

18) $\dfrac{6+i}{2-7i}$

Graphing Complex Numbers

✏️ *Identify each complex number graphed.*

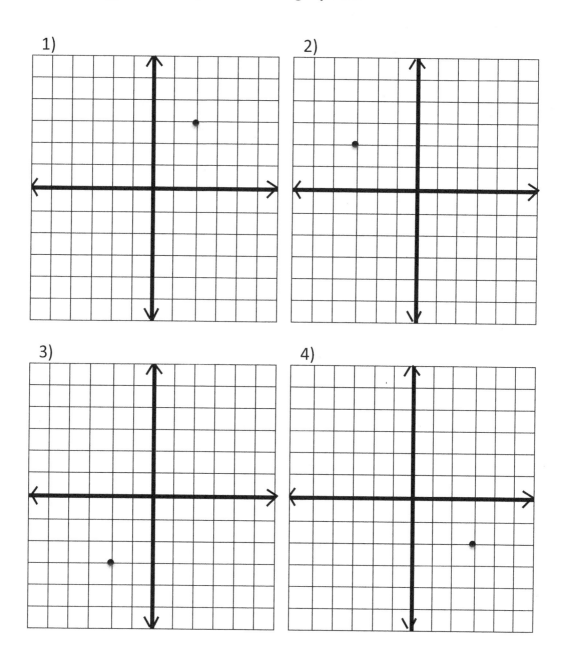

Rationalizing Imaginary Denominators

✍ Simplify.

1) $\dfrac{8-8i}{-4i}$

2) $\dfrac{2-10i}{-8i}$

3) $\dfrac{5+7i}{9i}$

4) $\dfrac{6i}{-1+2i}$

5) $\dfrac{7i}{-2-6i}$

6) $\dfrac{-10-5i}{-4+4i}$

7) $\dfrac{-2-6i}{6+8i}$

8) $\dfrac{-6-3i}{7-12i}$

9) $\dfrac{-1+i}{-7i}$

10) $\dfrac{-4-i}{i}$

11) $\dfrac{c}{ib}$

12) $\dfrac{-3-i}{6+4i}$

13) $\dfrac{-5+i}{-3i}$

14) $\dfrac{-8}{-i}$

15) $\dfrac{-4-i}{-1+4i}$

16) $\dfrac{-16-4i}{-4+4i}$

17) $\dfrac{8}{-6i}$

18) $\dfrac{-4i-1}{-1+3i}$

Answers of Worksheets – Chapter 1

Adding and Subtracting Integers

1) −19
2) −14
3) 6
4) 19
5) 19
6) −24
7) −52
8) 0
9) −10
10) −3
11) 9
12) 29
13) 26
14) −23
15) 34
16) 35
17) −25
18) 61
19) 5
20) 12
21) 45
22) 35
23) −3
24) 61

Multiplying and Dividing Integers

1) 28
2) 42
3) 84
4) 147
5) −168
6) −120
7) 72
8) 65
9) −168
10) −40
11) 63
12) −264
13) 7
14) −15
15) 9
16) −4
17) −19
18) 7
19) −37
20) −13
21) 9
22) 8
23) 6
24) 13

Arrange and Order, Comparing Integers

1) −17, −12, −1, 1, 12
2) −7, −3, 2, 5, 11
3) −52, −22, 0, 25, 19
4) −84, −55, −13, 0, 31, 47
5) −51, −45, −18, 21, 39, 42
6) −65, −51, −39, −25, −17, 71
7) 81, 77, 36, 24, 19, 5
8) 7, 4, −1, −3, −7

9) 37, 27, 17, − 17, − 47

10) 19, 15, − 14, − 17, −21

11) −3, −2, -1, 0,1,2

12) 31, 19, −28, −75, −91, −124

Compare.

1) <

2) >

3) >

4) >

5) <

6) >

7) <

8) >

9) =

10) >

Order of Operations

1) 17

2) 41

3) 40

4) 27

5) 12

6) 58

7) 2

8) 14

9) 95

10) −3

11) 1

12) 71

Integers and Absolute Value

1) 22

2) 12

3) 31

4) 0

5) 47

6) 9

7) 1

8) 37

9) 23

10) 4

11) 57

12) 19

13) 15

14) 55

15) 36

16) 93

17) − 80

18) 57

19) 43

20) 44

21) 20

22) 23

23) 18

24) −14

Adding and Subtracting Complex Numbers

1) $-12 + 8i$

2) $15 - 18i$

3) $-16 - 6i$

4) $-3 + 2i$

5) $13 + 5i$

6) $9 - i$

7) $7 - 4i$

8) $15 + 14i$

9) $6 - 6i$

10) $-2 + 12i$

11) $10 - 16i$

12) $-2 - 6i$

13) $-15 + 10i$

14) $4 + 5i$

15) $2 + 10i$

16) $8 - 16i$

Multiplying and Dividing Complex Numbers

1) $4 - 10i$

2) $-16 - 18i$

3) $-36 - 3i$

4) $1 + 55i$

5) $-5 + 12i$

6) $6 + 19i$

7) $\frac{40+18i}{140}$

8) $\frac{2}{3} + i$

9) $\frac{46}{65} - \frac{22}{65}i$

10) $\frac{18-i}{25}$

11) $-4i + 5$

12) $\frac{1}{5} - \frac{2}{5}i$

13) $\frac{2i}{9}$

14) $\frac{i-3}{2}$

15) $\frac{27i-9}{10}$

16) $-\frac{9}{61} - \frac{23i}{61}$

17) $-\frac{8}{13} + \frac{14i}{13}$

18) $\frac{5}{53} + \frac{44i}{53}$

Graphing Complex Numbers

1) $2 + 3i$

2) $-3 + 2i$

3) $-2 - 3i$

4) $3 - 2i$

Rationalizing Imaginary Denominators

1) $2i + 2$

2) $\frac{5+i}{4}$

3) $\frac{-7+5i}{9}$

4) $\frac{-6i+12}{5}$

5) $\frac{-7i-21}{20}$

6) $\frac{5+15i}{8}$

7) $\frac{-3-i}{5}$

8) $\frac{-6-93i}{193}$

9) $\frac{-i-1}{7}$

10) $4i - 1$

11) $-\frac{ic}{b}$

12) $\frac{-11+3i}{26}$

13) $\frac{-1-5i}{3}$

14) $-8i$

15) $0 + 1i$

16) $\frac{3+5i}{2}$

17) $\frac{4i}{3}$

18) $\frac{13i+1}{10}$

Chapter 2:

Fractions and Decimals

Topics that you'll learn in this chapter:

- Simplifying Fractions
- Adding and Subtracting Fractions, Mixed Numbers and Decimals
- Multiplying and Dividing Fractions, Mixed Numbers and Decimals
- Comparing and Rounding Decimals
- Converting Between Fractions, Decimals and Mixed Numbers
- Factoring Numbers, Greatest Common Factor, and Least Common Multiple
- Divisibility Rules

"A Man is like a fraction whose numerator is what he is and whose denominator is what he thinks of himself. The larger the denominator, the smaller the fraction."
–Tolstoy

Factoring Numbers

List all positive factors of each number.

1) 32

2) 26

3) 40

4) 96

5) 60

6) 28

7) 35

8) 64

9) 56

10) 75

11) 81

12) 48

List the prime factorization for each number.

13) 20

14) 65

15) 99

16) 42

17) 84

18) 30

19) 52

20) 105

21) 75

22) 48

23) 36

24) 31

25) 24

26) 54

Greatest Common Factor (GCF)

Find the GCF for each number pair.

1) 14, 28

2) 48, 36

3) 6, 18

4) 25, 15

5) 52, 39

6) 57, 38

7) 16, 12

8) 45, 60

9) 36, 72

10) 27, 63

11) 64, 48

12) 80, 45

13) 36, 42

14) 15, 90

15) 63, 84

16) 100, 75

17) 26, 42

18) 93, 62

Least Common Multiple (LCM)

Find the LCM for each number pair.

1) 6, 9

2) 25, 35

3) 64, 48

4) 12, 18

5) 14, 21

6) 45, 15

7) 42, 63

8) 21, 12

9) 64, 44

10) 15, 12

11) 75, 6

12) 20, 10, 40

13) 16, 32, 24

14) 15, 25, 35

15) 14, 8, 21

16) 5, 9, 7

17) 14, 6, 16

18) 36, 60, 24

Divisibility Rules

✏️ *Use the divisibility rules to find the factors of each number*

1) 24   2 3 4 5 6 7 8 9 10

2) 32   2 3 4 5 6 7 8 9 10

3) 16   2 3 4 5 6 7 8 9 10

4) 42   2 3 4 5 6 7 8 9 10

5) 28   2 3 4 5 6 7 8 9 10

6) 56   2 3 4 5 6 7 8 9 10

7) 48   2 3 4 5 6 7 8 9 10

8) 36   2 3 4 5 6 7 8 9 10

9) 81   2 3 4 5 6 7 8 9 10

10) 50   2 3 4 5 6 7 8 9 10

11) 63   2 3 4 5 6 7 8 9 10

12) 84   2 3 4 5 6 7 8 9 10

Simplifying Fractions

Simplify the fractions.

1) $\dfrac{42}{62}$

2) $\dfrac{18}{24}$

3) $\dfrac{10}{15}$

4) $\dfrac{36}{48}$

5) $\dfrac{9}{27}$

6) $\dfrac{20}{80}$

7) $\dfrac{12}{27}$

8) $\dfrac{28}{56}$

9) $\dfrac{40}{100}$

10) $\dfrac{7}{63}$

11) $\dfrac{25}{45}$

12) $\dfrac{24}{32}$

13) $5\dfrac{35}{56}$

14) $2\dfrac{35}{56}$

15) $9\dfrac{35}{56}$

16) $3\dfrac{35}{56}$

17) $1\dfrac{52}{64}$

18) $4\dfrac{13}{65}$

19) $1\dfrac{45}{60}$

20) $\dfrac{54}{60}$

21) $7\dfrac{66}{132}$

Adding and Subtracting Fractions

🖎 Add fractions.

1) $\dfrac{1}{3} + \dfrac{1}{2}$

2) $\dfrac{2}{7} + \dfrac{2}{3}$

3) $\dfrac{3}{7} + \dfrac{4}{9}$

4) $\dfrac{5}{12} + \dfrac{1}{3}$

5) $\dfrac{3}{6} + \dfrac{1}{5}$

6) $\dfrac{3}{15} + \dfrac{2}{5}$

7) $\dfrac{2}{7} + \dfrac{5}{7}$

8) $\dfrac{5}{13} + \dfrac{2}{4}$

9) $\dfrac{16}{56} + \dfrac{3}{16}$

🖎 Subtract fractions.

10) $\dfrac{3}{5} - \dfrac{1}{10}$

11) $\dfrac{5}{8} - \dfrac{2}{5}$

12) $\dfrac{5}{6} - \dfrac{2}{7}$

13) $\dfrac{1}{8} - \dfrac{1}{9}$

14) $\dfrac{3}{5} - \dfrac{5}{12}$

15) $\dfrac{5}{8} - \dfrac{5}{16}$

16) $\dfrac{2}{25} - \dfrac{1}{15}$

17) $\dfrac{3}{4} - \dfrac{13}{18}$

18) $\dfrac{8}{42} - \dfrac{7}{48}$

Multiplying and Dividing Fractions

Multiplying fractions. Then simplify.

1) $\dfrac{2}{7} \times \dfrac{3}{8}$

2) $\dfrac{4}{25} \times \dfrac{5}{8}$

3) $\dfrac{9}{40} \times \dfrac{10}{27}$

4) $\dfrac{6}{13} \times \dfrac{26}{33}$

5) $\dfrac{9}{12} \times \dfrac{4}{5}$

6) $\dfrac{12}{17} \times \dfrac{3}{5}$

7) $\dfrac{28}{115} \times 0$

8) $\dfrac{8}{9} \times \dfrac{9}{8}$

9) $\dfrac{14}{45} \times \dfrac{15}{28}$

Dividing fractions.

10) $0 \div \dfrac{1}{10}$

11) $\dfrac{5}{12} \div 5$

12) $\dfrac{6}{11} \div \dfrac{3}{4}$

13) $\dfrac{21}{32} \div \dfrac{7}{8}$

14) $\dfrac{4}{19} \div \dfrac{8}{19}$

15) $\dfrac{3}{16} \div \dfrac{15}{32}$

16) $\dfrac{5}{7} \div \dfrac{1}{6}$

17) $\dfrac{16}{25} \div \dfrac{4}{5}$

18) $\dfrac{2}{17} \div \dfrac{2}{13}$

19) $9 \div \dfrac{1}{6}$

20) $\dfrac{12}{28} \div \dfrac{3}{7}$

21) $\dfrac{6}{17} \div \dfrac{5}{14}$

22) $\dfrac{-7}{15} \div \dfrac{14}{30}$

23) $\dfrac{3}{5} \div \dfrac{9}{10}$

24) $\dfrac{57}{69} \div \dfrac{19}{115}$

Adding and Subtracting Mixed Numbers

✏️ Add.

1) $2\frac{1}{4} + 3\frac{1}{4}$

2) $5\frac{3}{4} + 2\frac{1}{4}$

3) $1\frac{1}{9} + 2\frac{2}{9}$

4) $3\frac{1}{6} + 2\frac{2}{3}$

5) $5\frac{4}{15} + 5\frac{3}{10}$

6) $4\frac{1}{7} + 1\frac{1}{3}$

7) $1\frac{5}{21} + 1\frac{5}{28}$

8) $3\frac{2}{5} + 1\frac{3}{7}$

9) $3\frac{3}{8} + 4\frac{1}{12}$

10) $12 + \frac{1}{8}$

11) $2\frac{5}{18} + \frac{5}{24}$

12) $4\frac{7}{16} + 1\frac{1}{2}$

✏️ Subtract.

1) $4\frac{3}{8} - 1\frac{1}{8}$

2) $3\frac{7}{12} - \frac{1}{3}$

3) $5\frac{9}{14} - 5\frac{6}{21}$

4) $11\frac{4}{9} - 7\frac{1}{4}$

5) $3\frac{1}{3} - 2\frac{2}{3}$

6) $7\frac{1}{8} - 2\frac{1}{2}$

7) $5\frac{4}{17} - 2\frac{4}{17}$

8) $4\frac{10}{11} - 2\frac{1}{3}$

9) $4\frac{2}{7} - 3\frac{2}{5}$

10) $4\frac{5}{9} - 2\frac{7}{18}$

11) $5\frac{7}{15} - 3\frac{2}{15}$

12) $6\frac{1}{21} - 2\frac{1}{35}$

Multiplying and Dividing Mixed Numbers

✎ Find each product.

1) $1\frac{1}{4} \times 1\frac{1}{4}$

2) $2\frac{3}{7} \times 1\frac{2}{3}$

3) $4\frac{3}{5} \times 3\frac{3}{4}$

4) $4\frac{1}{8} \times 1\frac{2}{5}$

5) $3\frac{2}{3} \times 2\frac{1}{5}$

6) $1\frac{1}{9} \times 1\frac{2}{3}$

7) $4\frac{1}{2} \times 1\frac{3}{8}$

8) $4\frac{1}{2} \times 2\frac{1}{5}$

9) $2\frac{2}{3} \times 3\frac{1}{4}$

10) $3\frac{1}{5} \times 3\frac{3}{4}$

11) $1\frac{1}{6} \times 1\frac{1}{3}$

12) $1\frac{5}{9} \times 1\frac{4}{5}$

✎ Find each quotient.

1) $2\frac{3}{5} \div 1\frac{3}{5}$

2) $4\frac{1}{6} \div 1\frac{2}{3}$

3) $3\frac{2}{5} \div 1\frac{2}{15}$

4) $3\frac{3}{4} \div 2\frac{5}{8}$

5) $1\frac{3}{7} \div 1\frac{1}{2}$

6) $2\frac{5}{6} \div 2\frac{2}{3}$

7) $2\frac{2}{3} \div 3\frac{1}{5}$

8) $3\frac{1}{5} \div 2\frac{2}{3}$

9) $2\frac{1}{7} \div 1\frac{3}{5}$

10) $2\frac{7}{12} \div 6\frac{1}{5}$

11) $3\frac{2}{7} \div 1\frac{5}{9}$

12) $0 \div 1\frac{1}{2}$

Comparing Decimals

Write the correct comparison symbol (>, < or =).

1) 1.15 ___ 2.15

2) 0.4 ___ 0.385

3) 12.5 ___ 12.500

4) 4.05 ___ 4.50

5) 0.511 ___ 0.51

6) 0.623 ___ 0.723

7) 8.76 ___ 8.678

8) 3.0069 ___ 3.069

9) 22.042 ___ 22.034

10) 5.11 ___ 5.08

11) 1.11 ___ 1.111

12) 0.06 ___ 0.55

13) 3.204 ___ 3.25

14) 3.92 ___ 3.0952

15) 0.44 ___ 0.044

16) 17.04 ___ 17.040

17) 0.090 ___ 0.80

18) 0.021 ___ 0.201

19) 0.0067 ___ 0.00089

20) 0.79 ___ 0.6

Rounding Decimals

Round each decimal number to the nearest place indicated.

1) 0.6̲3

2) 3.0̲4

3) 7.6̲23

4) 0.3̲66

5) 7̲.707

6) 0.08̲8

7) 6.2̲4

8) 76.76̲0

9) 3.62̲9

10) 12.3̲858

11) 1.0̲9

12) 4.2̲57

13) 3.2̲43

14) 6.05̲40

15) 93̲.69

16) 37̲.45

17) 41̲7.078

18) 312.6̲55

19) 18.40̲09

20) 85̲.85

21) 3.20̲8

22) 57.0̲73

23) 126.5̲18

24) 7.00̲69

25) 0.01̲11

26) 11.34̲06

27) 6.3̲891

{ 39 }

Adding and Subtracting Decimals

✍ *Add and subtract decimals.*

1) 37.69
   $-\ 15.58$
   _____

2) 56.93
   $+\ 23.07$
   _____

3) 18.96
   $+\ 12.87$
   _____

4) 84.10
   $-\ 43.45$
   _____

5) 121.26
   $+\ 78.97$
   _____

6) 65.00
   $-\ 53.39$
   _____

✍ *Solve.*

7) ___ + 3.3 = 5.08

8) 5.05 + ___ = 14.6

9) 12.9 − ___ = 7.25

10) 6.9 − ___ = 0.047

11) ___ + 0.074 = 1.084

12) ___ − 6.62 = 31.72

Multiplying and Dividing Decimals

Find each product

1) 5.5 × 2.6

2) 8.7 × 6.9

3) 4.06 × 7.05

4) 21.09 × 9.07

5) 14.3 × 15.7

6) 4.0 × 7.09

7) 6.9 × 0.8

8) 67.08 × 10

9) 12.08 × 1000

Find each quotient.

10) 18.7 ÷ 2.5

11) 45.2 ÷ 5

12) 15.6 ÷ 4.5

13) 8.05 ÷ 2.5

14) 7.6 ÷ 100

15) 2.07 ÷ 10

16) 7.38 ÷ 1000

17) 36.1 ÷ 100

18) 0.03 ÷ 10

Converting Between Fractions, Decimals and Mixed Numbers

✎ **Convert fractions to decimals**

1) $\dfrac{5}{10}$

2) $\dfrac{36}{100}$

3) $\dfrac{5}{8}$

4) $\dfrac{15}{16}$

5) $\dfrac{6}{18}$

6) $\dfrac{40}{100}$

7) $\dfrac{32}{40}$

8) $\dfrac{14}{25}$

9) $\dfrac{73}{10}$

✎ **Convert decimal into fraction or mixed numbers.**

10) 0.7

11) 7.25

12) 0.44

13) 5.3

14) 0.16

15) 0.05

16) 0.18

17) 0.4

18) 0.06

19) 0.68

20) 4.6

21) 3.2

Answers of Worksheets – Chapter 2

Factoring Numbers

1) 1, 2, 4, 8, 16, 32
2) 1, 2, 13, 26
3) 1, 2, 4, 5, 8, 10, 20, 40
4) 1, 2, 3, 4, 6, 8, 12 7, 16, 24, 32, 48, 96
5) 1, 2, 3, 4, 5, 6, 10, 12, 15, 20, 30, 60
6) 1, 2, 4, 7, 14, 28
7) 1, 5, 7, 35
8) 1, 2, 4, 8, 16, 32, 64
9) 1, 2, 4, 7, 8, 14, 56
10) 1, 3, 5, 15, 25, 75
11) 1, 3, 9, 27, 81
12) 1, 2, 3, 4, 6, 8, 12, 16, 24, 48
13) $2 \times 2 \times 5$
14) 5×13
15) $3 \times 3 \times 11$
16) $3 \times 2 \times 7$
17) $2 \times 2 \times 3 \times 7$
18) $3 \times 2 \times 5$
19) $2 \times 2 \times 13$
20) $3 \times 5 \times 7$
21) $3 \times 5 \times 5$
22) $2 \times 2 \times 2 \times 2 \times 3$
23) $2 \times 2 \times 3 \times 3$
24) 31×1
25) $2 \times 2 \times 2 \times 3$
26) $2 \times 3 \times 3 \times 3$

Greatest Common Factor

1) 7
2) 1
3) 12
4) 5
5) 13
6) 19
7) 4
8) 15
9) 36
10) 9
11) 16
12) 6
13) 5
14) 15
15) 21
16) 25
17) 2
18) 31

Least Common Multiple

1) 18
2) 175
3) 96
4) 36
5) 42
6) 45
7) 126
8) 84
9) 704
10) 60
11) 150
12) 40

13) 96   15) 168   17) 336
14) 525   16) 315   18) 360

Divisibility Rules

1) 24   <u>2</u> <u>3</u> <u>4</u> 5 <u>6</u> 7 <u>8</u> 9 10
2) 32   <u>2</u> 3 <u>4</u> 5 6 7 <u>8</u> 9 10
3) 16   <u>2</u> 3 <u>4</u> 5 6 7 <u>8</u> 9 10
4) 42   <u>2</u> <u>3</u> 4 5 <u>6</u> <u>7</u> 8 9 10
5) 28   <u>2</u> 3 <u>4</u> 5 6 <u>7</u> 8 9 10
6) 56   <u>2</u> 3 <u>4</u> 5 6 <u>7</u> <u>8</u> 9 10
7) 48   <u>2</u> 3 <u>4</u> 5 <u>6</u> 7 <u>8</u> 9 10
8) 36   <u>2</u> <u>3</u> <u>4</u> 5 <u>6</u> 7 8 <u>9</u> 10
9) 81   2 <u>3</u> 4 5 6 7 8 <u>9</u> 10
10) 50   <u>2</u> 3 4 <u>5</u> 6 7 8 9 <u>10</u>
11) 63   2 <u>3</u> 4 5 6 <u>7</u> 8 <u>9</u> 10
12) 84   <u>2</u> 3 <u>4</u> 5 <u>6</u> 7 8 9 10

Simplifying Fractions

1) $\frac{21}{31}$ 7) $\frac{4}{9}$ 13) $5\frac{5}{8}$ 19) $1\frac{3}{4}$

2) $\frac{3}{4}$ 8) $\frac{1}{2}$ 14) $2\frac{13}{16}$ 20) $\frac{9}{10}$

3) $\frac{2}{3}$ 9) $\frac{2}{5}$ 15) $9\frac{1}{5}$ 21) $7\frac{1}{2}$

4) $\frac{3}{4}$ 10) $\frac{1}{9}$ 16) $3\frac{4}{7}$

5) $\frac{1}{3}$ 11) $\frac{5}{9}$ 17) $1\frac{1}{2}$

6) $\frac{1}{4}$ 12) $\frac{3}{4}$ 18) $4\frac{5}{12}$

Adding and Subtracting Fractions

1) $\frac{5}{6}$ 2) $\frac{20}{21}$ 3) $\frac{55}{63}$

4) $\frac{3}{4}$

5) $\frac{7}{10}$

6) $\frac{3}{5}$

7) 1

8) $\frac{23}{26}$

9) $\frac{21}{56}$

10) $\frac{1}{2}$

11) $\frac{9}{40}$

12) $\frac{23}{42}$

13) $\frac{1}{72}$

14) $\frac{11}{60}$

15) $\frac{5}{16}$

16) $\frac{1}{75}$

17) $\frac{1}{36}$

18) $\frac{5}{112}$

Multiplying and Dividing Fractions

1) $\frac{3}{28}$

2) $\frac{1}{10}$

3) $\frac{1}{12}$

4) $\frac{4}{11}$

5) $\frac{3}{5}$

6) $\frac{36}{85}$

7) 0

8) 1

9) $\frac{1}{6}$

10) 0

11) $\frac{1}{12}$

12) $\frac{8}{11}$

13) $\frac{3}{4}$

14) $\frac{1}{2}$

15) $\frac{2}{5}$

16) $\frac{30}{7}$

17) $\frac{4}{5}$

18) $\frac{13}{17}$

19) 54

20) 1

21) $\frac{84}{85}$

22) -2

23) $\frac{2}{3}$

24) 5

Adding Mixed Numbers

1) $5\frac{1}{2}$

2) 8

3) $3\frac{1}{3}$

4) $5\frac{5}{6}$

5) $10\frac{17}{30}$

6) $5\frac{10}{21}$

7) $2\frac{5}{12}$

8) $4\frac{29}{35}$

9) $7\frac{11}{24}$

10) $2\frac{35}{72}$

11) $3\frac{3}{4}$

12) $5\frac{15}{16}$

Subtract Mixed Numbers

1) $3\frac{1}{4}$

2) $3\frac{1}{4}$

3) $\frac{5}{14}$

4) $4\frac{7}{36}$

5) $\frac{2}{3}$

6) $4\frac{5}{8}$

7) 3

8) $2\frac{19}{33}$

9) $\frac{31}{35}$

10) $2\frac{1}{6}$

11) $2\frac{1}{3}$

12) $4\frac{2}{35}$

Multiplying Mixed Numbers

1) $1\frac{9}{16}$

2) $4\frac{1}{21}$

3) $5\frac{10}{21}$

4) $16\frac{3}{7}$

5) $8\frac{1}{15}$

6) $1\frac{23}{27}$

7) $6\frac{3}{16}$

8) $9\frac{9}{10}$

9) $8\frac{2}{3}$

10) 12

11) $1\frac{5}{9}$

12) $2\frac{4}{5}$

Dividing Mixed Numbers

1) $1\frac{5}{8}$

2) $2\frac{1}{2}$

3) 3

4) $1\frac{3}{7}$

5) $\frac{20}{21}$

6) $1\frac{1}{16}$

7) $\frac{5}{6}$

8) $1\frac{1}{5}$

9) $1\frac{19}{56}$

10) $\frac{5}{12}$

11) $2\frac{11}{98}$

12) 0

Comparing Decimals

1) <

2) >

3) =

4) <

5) >

6) <

7) >

8) <

9) >

10) >

11) <

12) <

13) <

14) >

15) >

16) =

17) <

18) <

19) >

20) >

Rounding Decimals

1) 1.0

2) 3.0

3) 7.6

4) 0.4

5) 8

6) 0.09

7) 6.2

8) 76.76

9) 3.63

10) 12.4

11) 1.1

12) 4.3

13) 3.2
14) 6.05
15) 94
16) 37
17) 420
18) 312.7
19) 18.4
20) 86
21) 3.21
22) 57.1
23) 126.5
24) 7.01

Adding and Subtracting Decimals

1) 22.11
2) 80
3) 31.83
4) 40.65
5) 200.23
6) 11.61
7) 1.78
8) 9.55
9) 5.65
10) 6.583
11) 1.01
12) 38.34

Multiplying and Dividing Decimals

1) 14.3
2) 60.03
3) 28.623
4) 191.2863
5) 224.51
6) 28.09
7) 5.52
8) 670.8
9) 12080
10) 7.48
11) 9.04
12) 3.46...
13) 3.22
14) 0.207
15) 0.076
16) 0.00738
17) 0.361
18) 0.003

Converting Between Fractions, Decimals and Mixed Numbers

1) 0.5
2) 0.36
3) 0.625
4) 0.9375
5) 0.333...
6) 0.4
7) 0.8
8) 0.56
9) 7.3
10) $\frac{7}{10}$
11) $7\frac{1}{4}$
12) $\frac{11}{25}$
13) $5\frac{3}{10}$
14) $\frac{4}{25}$
15) $\frac{1}{20}$
16) $\frac{9}{50}$
17) $\frac{2}{5}$
18) $\frac{3}{50}$
19) $\frac{17}{25}$
20) $4\frac{3}{5}$
21) $3\frac{1}{5}$

Chapter 3:

Proportion, Ratio, Percent

Topics that you'll learn in this chapter:

- ✓ Writing and Simplifying Ratios
- ✓ Create a Proportion
- ✓ Similar Figures
- ✓ Ratio and Rates Word Problems
- ✓ Percentage Calculations
- ✓ Converting Between Percent, Fractions, and Decimals
- ✓ Percent Problems
- ✓ Percent of Increase and Decrease
- ✓ Simple interest
- ✓ Markup, Discount, and Tax

"Do not worry about your difficulties in mathematics. I can assure you mine are still greater." – Albert Einstein

Writing and Simplifying Ratios

✍ *Express each ratio as a rate and unite rate.*

1) 75 dollars for 5 chairs.

2) 169 miles on 7 gallons of gas.

3) 168 miles on 3 hours

4) 16 inches of snow in 24 hours

5) 42 dimes t0 126 dimes

6) 27 feet out of 81 feet

✍ *Express each ratio as a fraction in the simplest form.*

7) 17 cups to 51 cups

8) 24 cakes out of 60 cakes

9) 42 red desks out of 189 desks

10) 45 story books out of 72 books

11) 28 gallons to 40 gallons

12) 68 miles out of 100 miles

✍ *Reduce each ratio.*

1) 24: 42

2) 45: 15

3) 28: 36

4) 24: 26

5) 14: 56

6) 48: 60

7) 108: 252

8) 81: 45

9) 100: 25

10) 18: 32

11) 60: 10

12) 35: 45

13) 76: 57

14) 10: 100

15) 16: 40

16) 17: 34

17) 5: 25

18) 66: 39

Create a Proportion

✎ Create proportion from the given set of numbers

1) 2, 1, 8, 4
2) 7, 24, 56, 3
3) 21, 18, 63, 6
4) 11, 15, 22, 30
5) 5, 30, 75, 2
6) 9, 7, 54, 42
7) 32, 2, 16, 4
8) 63, 12, 9, 84
9) 10, 10, 100, 1

Similar Figures

✎ Each pair of figures is similar. Find the missing side.

1)

2)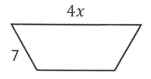

3)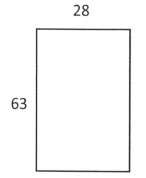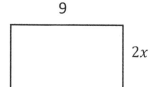

Ratio and Rates Word Problems

Solve.

1) In Peter's class, 27 of the students are tall and 15 are short. In Elise's class 81 students are tall and 45 students are short. Which class has a higher ratio of tall to short students?

2) In a party, 12 soft drinks are required for every 26 guests. If there are 364 guests, how many soft drinks is required?

3) The price of 6 bananas at the first Market is $1.08. The price of 4 of the same bananas at second Market is $0.76. Which place is the better buy?

4) You can buy 4 cans of green beans at a supermarket for $2.40. How much does it cost to buy 32 cans of green beans?

5) The bakers at a Bakery can make 132 bagels in 6 hours. How many bagels can they bake in 8 hours? What is that rate per hour?

Percentage Calculations

Calculate the percentages.

1) 25% of 38

2) 42% of 8

3) 15% of 15

4) 63% of 75

5) 4% of 50

6) 35% of 14

7) 18% of 3

8) 9% of 47

9) 10% of 100

10) 50% of 72

11) 75% of 60

12) 95% of 12

13) 80% of 30

14) 11% of 120

15) 1% of 210

16) 32% of 0

Solve.

17) What percentage of 40 is 2

18) 13.2 is what percentage of 88?

19) 38 is what percentage of 76?

20) Find what percentage of 85 is 22.1.

Percent Problems

Solve each problem.

1) 64% of what number is 16?

2) What is 70% of 140 inches?

3) What percent of 58 is 23.2?

4) 8 is 250% of what?

5) 18 is what percent of 20?

6) 34 is 40% of what?

7) 9 is what percent of 12?

8) 95% of 100 is what number?

9) Mia require 60% to pass. If she gets 240 marks and falls short by 60 marks, what were the maximum marks she could have got?

10) Jack scored 34 out of 40 marks in mathematics, 8 out of 10 marks in history and 78 out of 100 marks in science. In which subject his percentage of marks is the best?

Markup, Discount, and Tax

Find the selling price of each item.

1) Cost of a chair: $18.99, markup: 25%, discount: 8%, tax: 8%

2) Cost of computer: $1,490.00, markup: 60%

3) Cost of a pen: $2.50, markup: 60%, discount: 20%, tax: 5%

4) Cost of a puppy: $1,900, markup: 38%, discount: 15%

Simple Interest

Use simple interest to find the ending balance.

1) $3,200 at 13.7% for 2 years.

2) $280,000 at 3.75% for 15 years.

3) $2,000 at 1.9% for 5 years.

4) $14,700 at 5.8% for 3 years.

5) $47,500 at 0.5% for 16 months.

6) Emily puts $4,500 into an investment yielding 2.75% annual simple interest; she left the money in for six years. How much interest does Sara get at the end of those six years?

7) A new car, valued at $36,000, depreciates at 8.5% per year from original price. Find the value of the car 5 years after purchase.

8) $360 interest is earned on a principal of $1,800 at a simple interest rate of 5% interest per year. For how many years was the principal invested?

TSI Math Workbook

Converting Between Percent, Fractions, and Decimals

✏️ *Converting fractions to decimals.*

1) $\dfrac{40}{100}$ 4) $\dfrac{1}{10}$ 7) $\dfrac{40}{50}$

2) $\dfrac{28}{100}$ 5) $\dfrac{7}{20}$ 8) $\dfrac{25}{10}$

3) $\dfrac{4}{25}$ 6) $\dfrac{2}{100}$ 9) $\dfrac{6}{30}$

✏️ *Write each decimal as a percent.*

10) 0.25 15) 0.2

11) 1.2 16) 1.05

12) 0.015 17) 0.0275

13) 0.005 18) 0.0025

14) 0.725 19) 0.175

Answers of Worksheets – Chapter 3

Writing Ratios

1) $\frac{75 \text{ dollars}}{5 \text{ books}}$, 15.00 dollars per chair

2) $\frac{169 \text{ miles}}{7 \text{ gallons}}$, 29 miles per gallon

3) $\frac{168 \text{ miles}}{3 \text{ hours}}$, 56 miles per hour

4) $\frac{120" \text{ of snow}}{24 \text{ hours}}$, 5 inches of snow per hour

5) $\frac{126 \text{ dimes}}{42 \text{ dimes}}$, 3 per dime

6) $\frac{108 \text{ feet}}{27 \text{ feet}}$, 4 per foot

7) $\frac{1}{3}$ 9) $\frac{2}{9}$ 11) $\frac{7}{10}$

8) $\frac{2}{5}$ 10) $\frac{5}{8}$ 12) $\frac{17}{25}$

Reduce each Ratio

1) 4: 7   6) 4: 5   11) 6: 1   16) 1: 2

2) 3: 1   7) 3: 7   12) 7: 9   17) 1: 5

3) 7: 9   8) 9: 5   13) 4: 3   18) 22: 13

4) 12: 13   9) 4: 1   14) 1: 10

5) 1: 4   10) 9: 16   15) 2: 5

Create a Proportion

1) 1: 4 = 2: 8   4) 11: 22 = 15: 30   7) 2: 16 =4: 32

2) 3: 24 = 7: 56   5) 5: 75=2: 30   8) 9: 63 =12: 84

3) 6: 18 = 21: 63   6) 7: 42 =9: 54   9) 1: 10 =10: 100

Similar Figures

1) 6   2) 2   3) 2

Ratio and Rates Word Problems

1) The ratio for both classes is equal to 9 to 5.

2) 168

3) The price at the first Market is a better buy.

4) $19.20

5) 176, the rate is 22 per hour.

Percentage Calculations

1) 9.5	6) 4.9	11) 45	16) 0
2) 3.36	7) 0.54	12) 11.4	17) 5%
3) 2.25	8) 4.23	13) 24	18) 15%
4) 47.25	9) 10	14) 13.2	19) 50%
5) 2	10) 36	15) 2.1	20) 26%

Percent Problems

1) 25	4) 3.2	7) 75%	10) Mathematics
2) 98	5) 90%	8) 95	
3) 40%	6) 85	9) 500	

Markup, Discount, and Tax

1) $24.53	2) $2,384	3) $3.36	4) $2,228.70

Simple Interest

1) $4,076.80	4) $17,257.80	7) $20,700
2) $437,500.00	5) $51,300.00	8) 4 years
3) $2,190.00	6) $742.50	

Converting Between Percent, Fractions, and Decimals

1) 0.4	6) 0.02	11) 120%	16) 105%
2) 0.28	7) 0.8	12) 1.5%	17) 2.75%
3) 0.16	8) 2.5	13) 0.5%	18) 0.25%
4) 0.1	9) 0.2	14) 72.5%	19) 17.5%
5) 0.35	10) 25%	15) 20%	

Chapter 4: Sequences and Series

Topics that you'll learn in this chapter:

- ✓ Arithmetic Sequences
- ✓ Geometric Sequences
- ✓ Comparing Arithmetic and Geometric Sequences
- ✓ Finite Geometric Series
- ✓ Infinite Geometric Series

Mathematics is like checkers in being suitable for the young, not too difficult, amusing, and without peril to the state. — Plato

Arithmetic Sequences

✎ Given the first term and the common difference of an arithmetic sequence find the first five terms and the explicit formula.

1) $a_1 = 23$, $d = 2$

2) $a_1 = -10$, $d = -2$

3) $a_1 = 15$, $d = 10$

4) $a_1 = -30$, $d = -50$

✎ Given *a term in an arithmetic sequence and the common difference find the first five terms and the explicit formula.*

5) $a_{36} = -248$, $d = -6$

6) $a_{34} = 156$, $d = 5$

7) $a_{38} = -52.3$, $d = -1.1$

8) $a_{20} = -591$, $d = -30$

✎ Given a term in an arithmetic sequence and the common difference find the recursive formula and the three terms in the sequence after the last one given.

9) $a_{22} = -46$, $d = -2$

10) $a_{12} = 28.6$, $d = 1.2$

11) $a_{18} = 26.4$, $d = 1.1$

12) $a_{32} = -1.2$, $d = 0.6$

Geometric Sequences

Determine if the sequence is geometric. If it is, find the common ratio.

1) -1, 5, -25, 125, ...

2) $-3, -9, -27, -81, ...$

3) 3, 16, 23, 64, ...

4) $-2, -8, -16, -32, ...$

Given the first term and the common ratio of a geometric sequence find the first five terms and the explicit formula.

5) $a_1 = 0.6, r = -5$

6) $a_1 = 1, r = 3$

Given the recursive formula for a geometric sequence find the common ratio, the first five terms, and the explicit formula.

7) $a_n = a_{n-1} \cdot 2, a_1 = 3$

8) $a_n = a_{n-1} \cdot -2, a_1 = -2$

9) $a_n = a_{n-1} \cdot 5, a_1 = 1$

10) $a_n = a_{n-1} \cdot 2, a_1 = -3$

Given two terms in a geometric sequence find the 8th term and the recursive formula.

11) $a_4 = 216$ and $a_5 = -1296$

12) $a_5 = -32$ and $a_2 = -4$

Comparing Arithmetic and Geometric Sequences

☑ *For each sequence, state if it arithmetic, geometric, or neither.*

1) 1, 3, 6, 9, 12, …

2) 1, 4, 16, 64, 256, …

3) 4, 24, 64, 100, …

4) −28, −30, −32, −34, −36, …

5) −5, 15, −45, 135, −405, …

6) 40, 43, 46, 49, 52, …

7) 1, 4, 7, 10, 13, …

8) −34, −27, −20, −13, −6, …

9) $a_n = -145 + 200n$

10) $a_n = 16 + 3n$

11) $a_n = -2 \cdot (-3)^{n-1}$

12) $a_n = -23 + 4n$

13) $a_n = (3n)^2$

14) $a_n = -40 + 7n$

15) $a_n = -(-2)^{n-1}$

16) $a_n = 3 \cdot (-3)^{n-1}$

Finite Geometric Series

Evaluate the related series of each sequence.

1) $1, -6, 36, -216$

2) $4, 8, 16, 32, 64$

3) $7, -21, 61, -183$

4) $-2, 1, -\dfrac{1}{2}, \dfrac{1}{4}, -\dfrac{1}{8}$

Evaluate each geometric series described.

5) $1 + 5 + 25 + 125 \ldots, n = 6$

6) $1 - 3 + 9 - 27 \ldots, n = 9$

7) $-2 - 8 - 32 - 128 \ldots, n = 9$

8) $4 - 8 + 16 - 32 \ldots, n = 7$

9) $1 + \dfrac{1}{2} + \dfrac{1}{4} + \dfrac{1}{8} \ldots, n = 6$

10) $-5 - 5 - 5 - 5 \ldots, n = 12$

11) $\sum_{n=1}^{8} 2 \cdot (-3)^{n-1}$

12) $\sum_{n=1}^{10} 5 \cdot 2^{n-1}$

13) $\sum_{p=1}^{6} (-3) \cdot (-4)^{p-1}$

14) $\sum_{m=1}^{9} -3^{m-1} 6$

15) $\sum_{n=1}^{9} 3^{n-1} 6$

16) $\sum_{n=1}^{4} \left(\dfrac{1}{3}\right)^{n-1} 4$

17) $\sum_{n=1}^{6} 4^{n-1} + \sum_{j=1}^{7} -3^{j-1}$

18) $5 \sum_{n=1}^{8} 5^{n-1}$

Infinite Geometric Series

✎ Determine if each geometric series converges or diverges.

1) $a_1 = -1$, $r = 3$

2) $a_1 = -3$, $r = 4$

3) $a_1 = 5.5$, $r = 0.5$

4) $81 + 27 + 9 + 3 \ldots,$

5) $-3 + \dfrac{12}{5} - \dfrac{48}{25} + \dfrac{192}{125} \ldots,$

6) $\dfrac{128}{3125} - \dfrac{64}{625} + \dfrac{32}{125} - \dfrac{16}{25} \ldots,$

✎ Evaluate each infinite geometric series described.

7) $a_1 = 3$, $r = -\dfrac{1}{5}$

8) $a_1 = 1$, $r = -4$

9) $a_1 = 1$, $r = -3$

10) $a_1 = 3$, $r = \dfrac{1}{2}$

11) $1 + 0.5 + 0.25 + 0.125 + \ldots$

12) $1 - 0.6 + 0.36 - 0.216 \ldots,$

13) $81 - 27 + 9 - 3 \ldots,$

14) $3 + \dfrac{9}{4} + \dfrac{27}{16} + \dfrac{81}{64} \ldots,$

15) $\sum_{k=1}^{\infty} 4^{k-1}$

16) $\sum_{i=1}^{\infty} \left(\dfrac{1}{3}\right)^{i-1}$

Answers of Worksheets – Chapter 4

Arithmetic Sequences

1) First Five Terms: 23, 25, 27, 29, 31, Explicit: $a_n = 23 + 2(n-1)$

2) First Five Terms: −10, −12, −14, −16, −18, Explicit: $a_n = -10 - 2(n-1)$

3) First Five Terms: 15, 25, 35, 45, 55, Explicit: $a_n = 15 + 10(n-1)$

4) First Five Terms: −30, −80, −130, −180, −230,

   Explicit: $a_n = -30 - 50(n-1)$

5) First Five Terms: −38, −44, −50, −56, −62, Explicit: $a_n = -38 - 6(n-1)$

6) First Five Terms: −9, −4, 1, 6, 11, Explicit: $a_n = -9 + 5(n-1)$

7) First Five Terms: −11.6, −12.7, −13.8, −14.9, −16,

   Explicit: $a_n = -11.6 - 1.1(n-1)$

8) First Five Terms: −21, −51, −81, −111, −141,

   Explicit: $a_n = -21 - 30(n-1)$

9) Next 3 terms: −48, −50, −52, Recursive: $a_n = a_{n-1} - 2$, $a_1 = -4$

10) Next 3 terms: 29.8, 31, 32.2, Recursive: $a_n = a_{n-1} + 1.2$, $a_1 = 15.4$

11) Next 3 terms: 27.5, 28.6, 29.7, Recursive: $a_n = a_{n-1} + 1.1$, $a_1 = 7.7$

12) Next 3 terms: −0.6, 0, 0.6, Recursive: $a_n = a_{n-1} + 0.6$, $a_1 = -19.8$

Geometric Sequences

1) $r = -5$ 3) not geometric

2) $r = 3$ 4) not geometric

5) First Five Terms: 0.6, −3, 15, −75, 375; Explicit: $a_n = 0.6 \cdot (-5)^{n-1}$

6) First Five Terms: 1, 3, 9, 27, 81; Explicit: $a_n = 3^{n-1}$

7) Common Ratio: $r = 2$; First Five Terms: 3, 6, 12, 24. 48

   Explicit: $a_n = 3 \cdot 2^{n-1}$

8) Common Ratio: $r = -2$; First Five Terms: −2, 4, −8, 16, −32

   Explicit: $a_n = -2 \cdot (-2)^{n-1}$

9) Common Ratio: r = 5; First Five Terms: 1, 5, 25, 125, 625

   Explicit: $a_n = 1 \cdot 5^{n-1}$

10) Common Ratio: r = 2; First Five Terms: −3, −6, −12, −24, −48

    Explicit: $a_n = -3 \cdot 2^{n-1}$

11) $a_8 = -279936$, Recursive: $a_n = a_{n-1} \cdot -6$, $a_1 = 1$

12) $a_8 = -256$, Recursive: $a_n = a_{n-1} \cdot 2$, $a_1 = -2$

Comparing Arithmetic and Geometric Sequences

1) Neither
2) Geometric
3) Neither
4) Arithmetic
5) Geometric
6) Arithmetic
7) Neither
8) Arithmetic
9) Arithmetic
10) Arithmetic
11) Geometric
12) Arithmetic
13) Neither
14) Arithmetic
15) Geometric
16) Geometric

Finite Geometric

1) −185
2) 124
3) −140
4) $-\frac{11}{8}$
5) 3906
6) 4921
7) −174762
8) 172
9) 2
10) Undefined
11) −3280
12) 5115
13) 2457
14) 29526
15) 59046
16) 6
17) 1912
18) 488280

Infinite Geometric

1) Diverges
2) Diverges
3) Converges
4) Converges
5) Converges
6) Diverges
7) $\frac{5}{2}$
8) No sum
9) No sum
10) 6
11) 2
12) 0.625
13) $\frac{243}{4}$
14) 12
15) No sum
16) $\frac{3}{2}$

Chapter 5:

Exponents and Radicals

Topics that you'll learn in this chapter:

✓ Multiplication Property of Exponents

✓ Division Property of Exponents

✓ Powers of Products and Quotients

✓ Zero, Negative Exponents and Bases

✓ Simplifying Radical Expressions

✓ Simplifying Radical Expressions Involving Fractions

✓ Multiplying Radical Expressions

✓ Adding and Subtracting Radical Expressions

✓ Domain and Range of Radical Functions

✓ Solving Radical Equations

Mathematics is no more computation than typing is literature.
– John Allen Paulos

Multiplication Property of Exponents

Simplify.

1) $3^2 \times 3^2$

2) $4 \cdot 4^2 \cdot 4^2$

3) $2^2 \cdot 2^2$

4) $5x^3 \cdot x$

5) $14x^4 \cdot 2x$

6) $5x \cdot 2x^2$

7) $6x^4 \cdot 7x^4$

8) $4x^2 \cdot 6x^3y^4$

9) $8x^2y^5 \cdot 8xy^3$

10) $5xy^4 \cdot 4x^3y^3$

11) $(3x^2)^2$

12) $4x^5y^3 \cdot 5x^2y^3$

13) $7x^3 \cdot 10y^3x^5 \cdot 7yx^3$

14) $(x^4)^3$

15) $(3x^2)^4$

16) $8x^4y^5 \cdot 2x^2y^3$

Division Property of Exponents

Simplify.

1) $\dfrac{5^6}{5}$

2) $\dfrac{43}{43^{45}}$

3) $\dfrac{3^2}{3^3}$

4) $\dfrac{5^4}{5^2}$

5) $\dfrac{x}{x^{13}}$

6) $\dfrac{24x^3}{6x^4}$

7) $\dfrac{2x^{-5}}{11x^{-2}}$

8) $\dfrac{49x^8}{7x^3}$

9) $\dfrac{11x^6}{4x^7}$

10) $\dfrac{42x^2}{4x^3}$

11) $\dfrac{x}{10x^3}$

12) $\dfrac{x^3}{2x^5}$

13) $\dfrac{16x^3}{14x^6}$

14) $\dfrac{12x^3}{6y^8}$

15) $\dfrac{25xy^4}{x^6y^2}$

16) $\dfrac{2x^4}{7x}$

17) $\dfrac{32x^2y^8}{4x^3}$

18) $\dfrac{12x^4}{15x^7y^9}$

19) $\dfrac{yx^4}{10yx^8}$

20) $\dfrac{16x^4y}{9x^8y^2}$

21) $\dfrac{6x^8}{36x^8}$

Powers of Products and Quotients

Simplify.

1) $(x^3)^4$

2) $(2xy^4)^2$

3) $(6x^4)^2$

4) $(12x^5)^2$

5) $(2x^2y^4)^4$

6) $(3x^4y^4)^3$

7) $(4x^2y^2)^2$

8) $(5x^4y^3)^4$

9) $(4x^6y^8)^2$

10) $(15x\ 3x)^3$

11) $(x^9\ x^6)^3$

12) $(7x^{10}y^3)^3$

13) $(6x^3\ x^2)^2$

14) $(4x^3\ 5x)^2$

15) $(10x^{11}y^3)^2$

16) $(8x^7\ y^5)^2$

17) $(9x^4y^6)^5$

18) $(3x^4)^2$

19) $(3x\ 4y^3)^2$

20) $(7x^2y)^3$

21) $(14x^2y^5)^2$

Zero and Negative Exponents

🖊️ **Evaluate the following expressions.**

1) 3^4

2) 7^{-2}

3) 5^{-4}

4) 12^{-1}

5) 7^{-1}

6) 6^{-2}

7) 8^{-2}

8) 5^{-2}

9) 15^{-1}

10) 7^{-3}

11) 0^5

12) 10^{-7}

13) 4^{-4}

14) 4^{-2}

15) 2^{-3}

16) 3^{-4}

17) 6^{-1}

18) 7^3

19) 11^{-2}

20) $(\frac{3}{4})^{-2}$

21) $(\frac{1}{5})^{-2}$

22) $(\frac{1}{2})^{-6}$

23) $(\frac{2}{5})^{-2}$

24) 10^{-4}

25) 1^{-100}

Negative Exponents and Negative Bases

🖊️ **Simplify.**

1) -4^{-1}

2) $-5x^{-3}$

3) $\frac{x}{x^{-3}}$

4) $-\frac{a^{-6}}{b^{-2}}$

5) $\frac{5}{x^{-3}}$

6) $\frac{b}{-9c^{-4}}$

7) $-\frac{25n^{-2}}{10p^{-3}}$

8) $\frac{4ab^{-2}}{-3c^{-2}}$

9) $10x^2y^{-3}$

10) $(-\frac{1}{4})^{-2}$

11) $(-\frac{5}{4})^{-2}$

12) $(\frac{x}{3yz})^{-3}$

TSI Math Workbook

Writing Scientific Notation

✎ Write each number in scientific notation.

1) 81×10^5

2) 50

3) 0.0000008

4) 254000

5) 0.000225

6) 6.5

7) 0.00063

8) 89000000

9) 9000000

10) 85000000

11) 0.0000036

12) 0.00015

13) 0.008

14) 8600

15) 1960

16) 170000

17) 0.115

18) 0.05

Square Roots

✎ Find the value each square root.

1) $\sqrt{81}$

2) $\sqrt{0}$

3) $\sqrt{36}$

4) $\sqrt{64}$

5) $\sqrt{49}$

6) $\sqrt{1}$

7) $\sqrt{25}$

8) $\sqrt{9}$

9) $\sqrt{144}$

10) $\sqrt{121}$

11) $\sqrt{16}$

12) $\sqrt{256}$

13) $\sqrt{100}$

14) $\sqrt{169}$

15) $\sqrt{324}$

16) $\sqrt{90}$

17) $\sqrt{484}$

18) $\sqrt{529}$

Simplifying Radical Expressions

☛ *Simplify.*

1) $\sqrt{33x^2}$

2) $\sqrt{40x^2}$

3) $\sqrt{25x^3}$

4) $\sqrt{144a}$

5) $\sqrt{512v}$

6) $\sqrt{9x^2}$

7) $\sqrt{384}$

8) $\sqrt{162p^3}$

9) $\sqrt{125m^4}$

10) $\sqrt{693x^3y^3}$

11) $\sqrt{81x^3y^3}$

12) $\sqrt{9a^4b^3}$

13) $\sqrt{40x^3y^3}$

14) $3\sqrt{45x^2}$

15) $5\sqrt{60x^2}$

16) $4\sqrt{81a}$

17) $3\sqrt{8x^2y^3r}$

18) $4\sqrt{64x^2y^3z^4}$

Simplifying Radical Expressions Involving Fractions

✎ *Simplify.*

1) $\dfrac{2\sqrt{7r}}{\sqrt{m^4}}$

2) $\dfrac{6\sqrt{2}}{\sqrt{k}}$

3) $\dfrac{\sqrt{c}}{\sqrt{c}+\sqrt{d}}$

4) $\dfrac{5+\sqrt{3}}{2-\sqrt{3}}$

5) $\dfrac{2+\sqrt{7}}{6-\sqrt{5}}$

6) $\dfrac{3}{2+\sqrt{3}}$

7) $\dfrac{\sqrt{6}-\sqrt{4}}{\sqrt{4}-\sqrt{6}}$

8) $\dfrac{\sqrt{3}}{\sqrt{7}-2}$

9) $\dfrac{\sqrt{2}-\sqrt{6}}{\sqrt{2}+\sqrt{6}}$

10) $\dfrac{3\sqrt{5}+5}{2\sqrt{5}-3}$

11) $\dfrac{\sqrt{8a^5b^3}}{\sqrt{2ab^2}}$

12) $\dfrac{6\sqrt{20x^3}}{3\sqrt{5x}}$

Multiplying Radical Expressions

✍ *Simplify.*

1) $\sqrt{12x} \times \sqrt{12x}$

2) $-5\sqrt{27} \times -3\sqrt{3}$

3) $3\sqrt{45x^2} \times \sqrt{5x^2}$

4) $\sqrt{8x^2} \times \sqrt{12x^3}$

5) $-10\sqrt{8} \times \sqrt{5x^3}$

6) $5\sqrt{21} \times \sqrt{3}$

7) $\sqrt{3} \times -\sqrt{64}$

8) $-5\sqrt{16x^3} \times 4\sqrt{2x^2}$

9) $\sqrt{12}\,(2+\sqrt{3})$

10) $-3\sqrt{8}\,(2+\sqrt{8})$

11) $\sqrt{12x}\,(3-\sqrt{6x})$

12) $\sqrt{3x}\,(x^3+\sqrt{27})$

13) $\sqrt{15r}\,(2+\sqrt{3})$

14) $\sqrt{2v}\,(\sqrt{6}+\sqrt{10})$

15) $(-2\sqrt{6}+3)(\sqrt{6}-1)$

16) $(2-\sqrt{3})(-2+\sqrt{3})$

17) $(10-4\sqrt{5})(6-\sqrt{5})$

18) $(\sqrt{6}-\sqrt{3})(\sqrt{6}+\sqrt{3})$

Adding and Subtracting Radical Expressions

✏️ *Simplify.*

1) $6\sqrt{10} + 4\sqrt{10}$

2) $3\sqrt{12} - 3\sqrt{27}$

3) $-3\sqrt{22} - 5\sqrt{22}$

4) $-9\sqrt{7} + 12\sqrt{7}$

5) $6\sqrt{3} - \sqrt{27}$

6) $-\sqrt{18} + 4\sqrt{2}$

7) $-4\sqrt{7} + 4\sqrt{7}$

8) $3\sqrt{27} + 3\sqrt{3}$

9) $2\sqrt{20} - 2\sqrt{5}$

10) $3\sqrt{18} - \sqrt{2}$

11) $-10\sqrt{35} + 14\sqrt{35}$

12) $-4\sqrt{19} - 5\sqrt{19}$

13) $-3\sqrt{6x} - 3\sqrt{6x}$

14) $\sqrt{5y^2} + y\sqrt{20}$

15) $\sqrt{8mn^2} + n\sqrt{18m}$

16) $-8\sqrt{27a} - 2\sqrt{3a}$

17) $-6\sqrt{7ab} - 6\sqrt{7ab}$

18) $\sqrt{27a^2b} + a\sqrt{12b}$

Solving Radical Equations

✎ **Solve each equation. Remember to check for extraneous solutions.**

1) $\sqrt{x-6} = 3$

2) $2 = \sqrt{x-3}$

3) $\sqrt{r} = 5$

4) $\sqrt{m+8} = 4$

5) $5\sqrt{3x} = 15$

6) $1 = \sqrt{x-4}$

7) $-18 = -6\sqrt{r+3}$

8) $10 = 2\sqrt{35v}$

9) $\sqrt{n+3} - 1 = 6$

10) $\sqrt{3r} = \sqrt{3r-2}$

11) $\sqrt{3x+15} = \sqrt{x+5}$

12) $\sqrt{v} = \sqrt{2v-5}$

13) $\sqrt{12-x} = \sqrt{x-2}$

14) $\sqrt{m+5} = \sqrt{3m+5}$

15) $\sqrt{2r+20} = \sqrt{-16-2r}$

16) $\sqrt{k+5} = \sqrt{1-k}$

17) $-10\sqrt{x-10} = -50$

18) $\sqrt{36-x} = \sqrt{\dfrac{x}{5}}$

Domain and Range of Radical Functions

Identify the domain and range of each.

1) $y = \sqrt{x + 4} - 3$

2) $y = \sqrt[3]{x - 3} + 6$

3) $y = \sqrt{x - 2} - 2$

4) $y = \sqrt[3]{x + 1} - 5$

Sketch the graph of each function.

5) $y = \sqrt{x} + 2$

6) $y = 3\sqrt{-x} - 2$

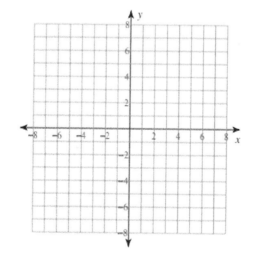
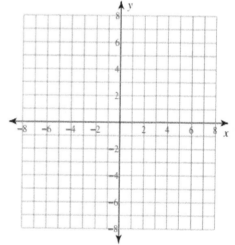

Answers of Worksheets – Chapter 5

Multiplication Property of Exponents

1) 3^4
2) 4^5
3) 2^4
4) $5x^4$
5) $48x^5$
6) $10x^3$
7) $42x^8$
8) $24x^5y^4$
9) $64x^3y^8$
10) $20x^4y^7$
11) $9x^4$
12) $20x^7y^6$
13) $490x^{11}y^4$
14) x^{12}
15) $81x^8$
16) $16x^6y^8$

Division Property of Exponents

1) 5^5
2) $\frac{1}{43^{44}}$
3) $\frac{1}{3}$
4) 5^2
5) $\frac{1}{x^{12}}$
6) $\frac{1}{4x}$
7) $\frac{2}{11x^3}$
8) $7x^5$
9) $\frac{11}{4x}$
10) $\frac{21}{2x}$
11) $\frac{1}{10x^2}$
12) $\frac{1}{2x^2}$
13) $\frac{8}{7x^3}$
14) $\frac{2x^3}{y^8}$
15) $\frac{25y^2}{x^5}$
16) $\frac{2x^3}{7}$
17) $\frac{8y^8}{x}$
18) $\frac{4}{5x^3y^9}$
19) $\frac{1}{10x^4}$
20) $\frac{16}{9x^4y}$
21) $\frac{1}{6}$

Powers of Products and Quotients

1) x^{12}
2) $4x^2y^8$
3) $36x^8$
4) $124x^{10}$
5) $16x^8y^{16}$
6) $27x^{12}y^{12}$
7) $16x^4y^4$
8) $625x^{16}y^{12}$
9) $16x^{12}y^{16}$
10) $3{,}375x^6$
11) x^{45}
12) $343x^{30}y^9$
13) $36x^{10}$
14) $350x^8$
15) $100x^{22}y^6$
16) $64x^{14}y^{10}$
17) $59{,}049x^{20}y^{30}$
18) $9x^8$
19) $144x^2y^6$
20) $343x^6y^3$
21) $196x^4y^{10}$

Zero and Negative Exponents

1) 81
2) $\frac{1}{49}$
3) $\frac{1}{324}$
4) $\frac{1}{12}$
5) $\frac{1}{7}$

6) $\frac{1}{36}$
7) $\frac{1}{16}$
8) $\frac{1}{64}$
9) $\frac{1}{15}$
10) $\frac{1}{343}$
11) 0
12) $\frac{1}{10000000}$
13) $\frac{1}{256}$
14) $\frac{1}{16}$
15) $\frac{1}{8}$
16) $\frac{1}{81}$
17) $\frac{1}{6}$
18) 343
19) $\frac{1}{121}$
20) $\frac{16}{9}$
21) 25
22) 64
23) $\frac{25}{4}$
24) $\frac{1}{10000}$
25) 1

Negative Exponents and Negative Bases

1) $-\frac{1}{4}$
2) $-\frac{5}{x^3}$
3) x^4
4) $-\frac{b^2}{a^6}$
5) $5x^3$
6) $-\frac{bc^4}{9}$
7) $-\frac{5p^3}{2n^2}$
8) $-\frac{4ac^2}{3b^2}$
9) $\frac{10x^2}{y^3}$
10) 16
11) $\frac{16}{25}$
12) $\frac{27y^3z^3}{x^3}$

Writing Scientific Notation

1) 8.1×10^6
2) 5×10^1
3) 8×10^{-7}
4) 2.54×10^5
5) 2.25×10^{-4}
6) 6.5×10^0
7) 6.3×10^{-4}
8) 8.9×10^7
9) 9×10^6
10) 8.5×10^7
11) 3.6×10^{-6}
12) 1.5×10^{-4}
13) 8×10^{-3}
14) 8.6×10^3
15) 1.96×10^3
16) 1.7×10^5
17) 1.15×10^{-1}
18) 5×10^{-2}

Square Roots

1) 9
2) 0
3) 6
4) 8
5) 7
6) 1
7) 5
8) 3
9) 12
10) 11
11) 4
12) 16
13) 10
14) 13
15) 18
16) 30
17) 22
18) 23

Simplifying radical expressions

1) $\sqrt{33}\,x$
2) $2x\sqrt{10}$
3) $5x\sqrt{x}$

4) $12\sqrt{a}$

5) $8\sqrt{8v}$

6) $3x$

7) $8\sqrt{6}$

8) $9p\sqrt{2p}$

9) $5m^2\sqrt{5}$

10) $3x.y\sqrt{77xy}$

11) $9x.y\sqrt{xy}$

12) $3a^2.b\sqrt{b}$

13) $2x.y\sqrt{10xy}$

14) $9x\sqrt{5}$

15) $10x\sqrt{15}$

16) $36\sqrt{a}$

17) $6x.y\sqrt{2qr}$

18) $32z^2.x.y\sqrt{y}$

Simplifying radical expressions involving fractions

1) $\frac{2\sqrt{7r}}{m^2}$

2) $\frac{6\sqrt{2k}}{k}$

3) $\frac{c-\sqrt{cd}}{c-d}$

4) $13+7\sqrt{3}$

5) $\frac{2\sqrt{7}+6\sqrt{5}}{31}$

6) $6-3\sqrt{3}$

7) $\frac{\sqrt{6}-1}{5}$

8) $\frac{\sqrt{21}+2\sqrt{3}}{3}$

9) $2+\sqrt{3}$

10) $\frac{19\sqrt{5}+45}{11}$

11) $2a^2\sqrt{b}$

12) $4x$

Multiplying radical expressions

1) $12x^2$

2) 135

3) $45x^2$

4) $4x^2.\sqrt{6x}$

5) $-20x^2.\sqrt{10}$

6) $15.\sqrt{7}$

7) $-8\sqrt{3}$

8) $-80x^2\sqrt{2x}$

9) $4\sqrt{3}+6$

10) $-(12\sqrt{2}+24)$

11) $6\sqrt{3x}-6x\sqrt{2}$

12) $\sqrt{3}.x^2+9x$

13) $3r\sqrt{5}+2\sqrt{15}\ r$

14) $2\sqrt{3v}+2\sqrt{5v}$

15) $5\sqrt{6}-15$

16) $4\sqrt{3}-7$

17) $-34\sqrt{5}+55$

18) 3

Adding and subtracting radical expressions

1) $10\sqrt{10}$

2) $-15\sqrt{3}$

3) $-8\sqrt{22}$

4) $3\sqrt{7}$

5) $3\sqrt{3}$

6) $\sqrt{2}$

7) 0

8) $12\sqrt{3}$

9) $2\sqrt{5}$

10) $8\sqrt{2}$

11) $4\sqrt{35}$

12) $-9\sqrt{19}$

13) $-6\sqrt{6x}$

14) $3y\sqrt{5}$

15) $5n\sqrt{2m}$

16) $-26\sqrt{3}\,a$

17) $-12\sqrt{7ab}$

18) $5a\sqrt{3b}$

Solving radical equations

1) {15}

2) {9}

3) {25}

4) {24}

5) {3}

6) {5}

7) {0}

8) {$\frac{5}{7}$}

9) {46}

10) {2}

11) {−5}

12) {5}

13) {7}

14) {0}

15) {−9}

16) {−2}

17) {35}

18) {30}

Domain and range of radical functions

1) domain: x ≥ −4

   range: y ≥ −3

2) domain: {all real numbers}

   range: {all real numbers}

3) domain: x ≥ 3

   range: y ≥ 6

4) domain: {all real numbers}

   range: {all real numbers}

5)

6)

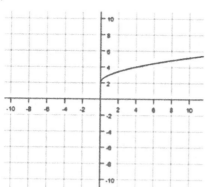

Chapter 6: Logarithms

Topics that you'll learn in this chapter:

- ✓ Rewriting Logarithms
- ✓ Evaluating Logarithms
- ✓ Properties of Logarithms
- ✓ Natural Logarithms
- ✓ Solving Exponential Equations Requiring Logarithms
- ✓ Solving Logarithmic Equations

Mathematics is an art of human understanding. – William Thurston

Rewriting Logarithms

✏️ *Rewrite each equation in exponential form.*

1) $\log_{23} 12 = 0.79$
2) $\log_{340} 25 = 0.55$
3) $\log_8 64 = 2$
4) $\log_{10} 100 = 2$

✏️ *Rewrite each equation in exponential form.*

5) $\log_a \frac{6}{7} = b$
6) $\log_x y = 8$
7) $\log_{15} n = m$
8) $\log_y x = -9$
9) $\log_a b = 33$
10) $\log_{\frac{1}{3}} v = u$

✏️ *Evaluate each expression.*

11) $\log_3 27$
12) $\log_6 216$
13) $\log_5 25$
14) $\log_8 4$

Evaluating Logarithms

✏️ *Evaluate each expression.*

1) $\log_2 16$
2) $\log_3 81$
3) $\log_2 8$
4) $\log_3 9$
5) $\log_9 81$
6) $\log_6 \frac{1}{36}$
7) $\log_{27} \frac{1}{3}$
8) $\log_{80} 300$
9) $\log_5 \frac{1}{125}$
10) $\log_4 256$
11) $\log_7 343$
12) $\log_3 \frac{1}{27}$
13) $\log_9 729$
14) $\log_8 4096$

Properties of Logarithms

Expand each logarithm.

1) $\log \left(\frac{4}{5}\right)^3$

2) $\log (7.3^3)$

3) $\log \left(\frac{5}{7}\right)^2$

4) $\log \frac{3^3}{5}$

5) $\log (x \cdot y)^7$

6) $\log (3 \cdot 8)$

7) $\log (2 \cdot 5)$

8) $\log (x^4 \cdot y \cdot z^5)$

9) $\log \frac{u^3}{v}$

10) $\log \frac{x}{y^9}$

Condense each expression to a single logarithm.

11) $\log 4 - \log 7$

12) $4 \log 3 - 3 \log 2$

13) $\log 5 - 3 \log 11$

14) $5 \log_7 a + 9 \log_7 b$

15) $2 \log_2 x - 5 \log_2 y$

16) $\log_6 u - 7 \log_6 v$

17) $2 \log_6 u + 5 \log_6 v$

18) $6 \log_5 u - 10 \log_5 v$

Natural Logarithms

Solve.

1) $e^x = 2$

2) $\ln (\ln x) = 7$

3) $e^x = 6$

4) $\ln (5x + 6) = 4$

5) $\ln (9x - 1) = 1$

6) $\ln x = \frac{1}{3}$

7) $x = e^{\frac{1}{2}}$

8) $\ln x = \ln 3 + \ln 8$

TSI Math Workbook

✎ *Evaluate without using a calculator.*

9) $\ln \sqrt{e}$

10) $\ln e^5$

11) $6 \ln e$

12) $\ln \left(\frac{1}{e}\right)$

13) $e^{\ln 12}$

14) $e^{3\ln 3}$

15) $e^{4\ln 2}$

16) $\ln 1$

Solving Exponential Equations Requiring Logarithms

✎ *Solve each equation.*

1) $2^{r+1} = 1$

2) $216^x = 36$

3) $4^{-3v-3} = 16$

4) $4^{2n} = 16$

5) $\frac{216^{2a}}{36^{-a}} = 216$

6) $24 \cdot 24^{-v} = 576$

7) $2^{2n} = 4$

8) $\left(\frac{1}{7}\right)^n = 49$

9) $32^{2x} = 4$

10) $2^{-2x} = 2^{x-1}$

11) $2^{2n} = 64$

12) $6^{3n} = 216$

13) $4^{-2k} = 256$

14) $6^{2r} = 6^{3r}$

15) $10^{5x} = 10000$

16) $36 \cdot 6^{-v} = 216$

17) $\frac{64}{16^{-3m}} = 16^{-2m-2}$

18) $3^{-2n} \cdot 3^{n+1} = 3^{-2n}$

Solving Logarithmic Equations

✏️ *Solve each equation.*

1) $2\log_6 - 2x = 0$

2) $-\log_2 3x = 2$

3) $\log x + 6 = 3$

4) $\log x - \log 2 = 1$

5) $\log x + \log 2 = 2$

6) $\log 5 + \log x = 1$

7) $\log x + \log 8 = \log 16$

8) $-2\log_2 (x - 3) = -10$

9) $\log 7x = \log (x + 6)$

10) $\log(9k - 5) = \log(3k - 1)$

11) $\log(5p - 1) = \log(-4p + 6)$

12) $-10 + \log_3(n + 2) = -10$

13) $\log_8(x + 3) = \log_8(x^2 + 30)$

14) $\log_{12}(v^2 + 34) = \log_{12}(-2v - 2)$

15) $\log(12 + 2b) = \log(b^2 - 2b)$

16) $\log_8(x + 4) - \log_8 x = \log_8 2$

17) $\log_2 4 + \log_2 x^2 = \log_2 36$

18) $\log_8(x + 1) - \log_8 x = \log_8 32$

Answers of Worksheets – Chapter 6

Rewriting Logarithms

1) $23^{0.79} = 12$
2) $340^{0.55} = 26$
3) $87^2 = 64$
4) $10^2 = 100$
5) $a^b = \frac{6}{7}$
6) $x^8 = y$
7) $15^m = n$
8) $y^{-9} = x$
9) $a^{33} = b$
10) $(\frac{1}{3})^u = v$
11) 3
12) 3
13) 2
14) $\frac{2}{3}$

Evaluating Logarithms

1) 4
2) 4
3) 3
4) 2
5) 2
6) –2
7) $-\frac{1}{3}$
8) 1.3
9) –3
10) 4
11) 3
12) –3
13) 3
14) 4

Properties of Logarithms

1) $3 \log 4 - 3 \log 5$
2) $\log 7 + 3 \log 3$
3) $2\log 5 - 2 \log 7$
4) $3 \log 3 - \log 5$
5) $7 \log x + 7 \log y$
6) $\log 3 + \log 8$
7) $\log 2 + \log 5$
8) $4\log x + \log y + 5 \log z$
9) $3 \log u - \log v$
10) $\log x - 9 \log y$
11) $\log \frac{4}{7}$
12) $\log \frac{3^4}{2^3}$
13) $\log \frac{5}{11^3}$
14) $\log_7 (a^5 b^9)$
15) $\log_2 \frac{x^2}{y^5}$
16) $\log_6 \frac{u}{v^7}$
17) $\log_6 (v^5 u^2)$
18) $\log_5 \frac{u^6}{v^{10}}$

Natural Logarithms

1) $x = \ln 2$
2) $x = e^{e^7}$
3) $x = \ln 6$

4) $x = \frac{e^2-6}{5}$
5) $x = \frac{e+1}{9}$
6) $x = e^{\frac{1}{3}}$
7) $x = e^e$
8) $x = 24$
9) $\frac{1}{2}$
10) 5
11) 6
12) −1
13) 12
14) 27
15) 16
16) 0

Solving Exponential Equations Requiring Logarithms

1) −1
2) $\frac{2}{3}$
3) $-\frac{5}{3}$
4) 1
5) $\{\frac{3}{8}\}$
6) −1
7) 1
8) −2
9) $\frac{1}{5}$
10) $\frac{1}{3}$
11) 3
12) 1
13) −2
14) 0
15) $\frac{4}{5}$
16) −1
17) $-\frac{7}{10}$
18) −1

Solving Logarithmic Equations

1) $\{-\frac{1}{2}\}$
2) $\{\frac{1}{12}\}$
3) {−1000}
4) {20}
5) {50}
6) {2}
7) {2}
8) {35}
9) {1}
10) $\{\frac{2}{3}\}$
11) $\{\frac{7}{9}\}$
12) {−1}
13) {−9, −3}
14) {−9}
15) {6, −2}
16) {4}
17) {3, −3}
18) $\{\frac{1}{31}\}$

Chapter 7:

Linear Functions

Topics that you'll learn in this chapter:

- ✓ Relations and Functions
- ✓ Adding and Subtracting Functions
- ✓ Multiplying and Dividing Functions
- ✓ Finding Slope and Rate of Change
- ✓ Find the X–intercept and Y–intercept
- ✓ Graphing Lines Using Slope–Intercept Form
- ✓ Graphing Lines Using Standard Form
- ✓ Writing Linear Equations
- ✓ Write an Equation from a Graph
- ✓ Equations of horizontal and vertical lines
- ✓ Equation of parallel or perpendicular lines

"Without mathematics, there's nothing you can do. Everything around you are mathematics. Everything around you are numbers." – Shakuntala Devi

Relation and Functions

State the domain and range of each relation. Then determine whether each relation is a function.

1) Function: ....

Domain:

....

Range:

....

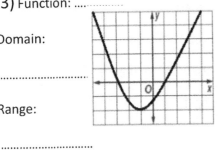

2) Function:

....

Domain:

....

Range:

....

x	y
2	2
0	0
−1	−1
4	−1
5	1

3) Function: ....

Domain:

....

Range:

....

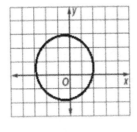

4) $\{(2, -1), (3, -2), (0, 1), (3, 0), (1, 1)\}$

Function: ....

Domain:

....

Range:

....

5) Function:

....

Domain:

....

Range:

....

6) Function:

....

Domain:

....

Range:

....

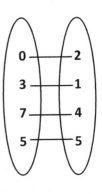

Slope and Rate of Change

Find the slope of the line through each pair of points.

1) $(4,1),(2,5)$

2) $(1,-6),(-5,3)$

3) $(2,-7),(5,-8)$

4) $(12,9),(18,14)$

5) $(0,-3),(7,-2)$

6) $(11,-7),(13,-5)$

7) $(-3,-5),(-11,-1)$

8) $(0,0),(6,-1)$

9) $(16,-9),(-4,4)$

10) $(-8,6),(-8,2)$

11) $(-12,-7),(-4,-13)$

12) $(-14,0),(0,-14)$

Write the slope–intercept form of the equation of the line through the given points.

1) Through: $(5,3),(7,2)$

2) Through: $(-4,-5),(-3,-2)$

3) Through: $(0.5,1),(2,1.4)$

4) Through: $(9,-4),(2.5,1)$

5) Through: $(-1,0),(-2,7)$

6) Through: $(7,-6),(2,9)$

7) Through: $(9,4),(7,3)$

8) Through: $(-0.5,1),(5,-1)$

9) Through: $(4,-3),(8,9)$

10) Through: $(1,5),(-2,5)$

11) Through: $(2,4),(-1,-2)$

12) Through: $(8,6),(0,-2)$

Find the value of b: The line that passes through each pair of points has the given slope.

1) $(3, -2), (1, b), m = 1$

2) $(b, -6), (-3, 8), m = -1\frac{2}{5}$

3) $(-3, b), (3, 7), m = \frac{1}{3}$

4) $(0, 2), (b, 5), m = -\frac{1}{3}$

Write the slope intercept form of the equation of each line

1)
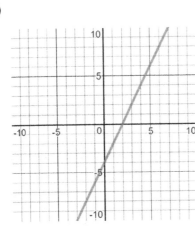

2)
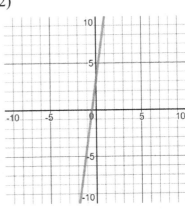

3)
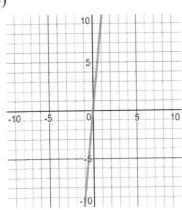

4)
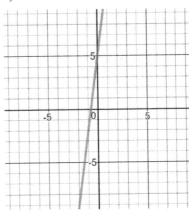

Rate of change

❧ **What is the average rate of change of the function?**

1) $f(x) = 2x^2 + 3$, from $x = 3$ to $x = 7$?
2) $f(x) = -x^2 - 2$, from $x = 0$ to $x = 2$?
3) $f(x) = x^3 + 1$, from $x = 1$ to $x = 3$?

xandy intercepts

❧ Find the x and y intercepts for the following equations.

1) $3x + 2y = 12$ 2) $y = x + 7$ 3) $3x = y + 15$

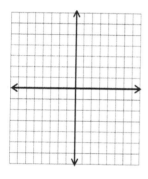 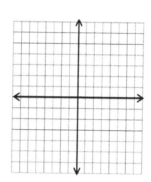 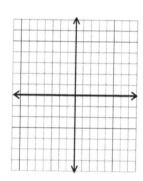

4) $x + y = 0$ 5) $7x - 3y = 5$ 6) $5y - 4x + 8 = 0$

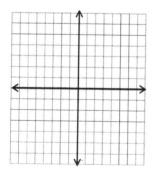 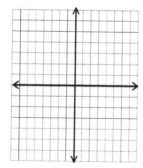 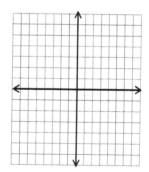

Slope–intercept Form

Write the slope–intercept form of the equation of each line.

1) $-12x + y = 5$

2) $-3(5x + y) = 45$

3) $-7x - 14y = -42$

4) $6x + 25 = -4y$

5) $x - 2y = 8$

6) $21x - 15y = -9$

7) $32x - 16y = -64$

8) $9x - 6y + 27 = 0$

9) $-\frac{2}{7}y = -3x + 1$

10) $7 - y - 3x = 0$

11) $-y = -3x - 8$

12) $8x + 4y = -16$

13) $2(x + y + 5) = 0$

14) $y - 5 = x + 6$

15) $4(y + 3) = 5(x - 3)$

16) $\frac{2}{3}y + \frac{1}{3}x + \frac{4}{3} =$

Point–slope Form

✍ Find the slope of the following lines. Name a point on each line.

1) $y = 3(x + 2)$

2) $y + 5 = \dfrac{2}{3}(x - 2)$

3) $y + 1 = -2.5x$

4) $y - 5 = \dfrac{1}{2}(x - 4)$

5) $y + 2 = 1.4(x + 2)$

6) $y - 7 = -4x$

7) $y - 10 = -4(x - 6)$

8) $y + 15 = 0$

9) $y + 8 = 3(x + 1)$

10) $y - 11 = -7(x - 3)$

✍ Write an equation in point–slope form for the line that passes through the given point with the slope provided.

11) $(2, -1), m = 5$

12) $(-2, 4), m = \dfrac{1}{2}$

13) $(0, -8), m = -1$

14) $(a, b), m = m$

15) $(-5, 3), m = 5$

16) $(2, 0), m = -6$

17) $(-6, 8), m = \dfrac{2}{3}$

18) $(-1, 12), m = 0$

19) $\left(-\dfrac{1}{4}, 2\right), m = \dfrac{1}{8}$

20) $(0, 0), m = -4$

Equation of Parallel or Perpendicular Lines

✎ Write an equation of the line that passes through the given point and is parallel to the given line.

1) $(-2,-4), 2x + 3y = -6$

2) $(-3,0), y = x - 3$

3) $(-1,0), 3y = 7x - 2$

4) $(0,0), -2y + 6x - 15 = 0$

5) $(2,13), y + 17 = 0$

6) $(0,5), -8x - y = -7$

7) $(-3,-2), y = \frac{3}{4}x + 2$

8) $(-1,3), -6x + 5y = -17$

9) $(5,-3), y = -\frac{3}{5}x - 2$

10) $(-4,-4), 9x + 12y = -24$

✎ Write an equation of the line that passes through the given point and is perpendicular to the given line.

11) $(-2,-5), 2x + 3y = -9$

12) $(-\frac{1}{2},\frac{3}{4}), 3x - 9y = -24$

13) $(3,-7), y = -7$

14) $(8,-4), x = 8$

15) $(0,-4), y = \frac{1}{3}x + 5$

16) $(\frac{2}{5},\frac{4}{5}), y = -4x - 21$

17) $(-6,0), y = \frac{3}{2}x - 13$

18) $(1,-3), y = x + 15$

19) $(-2,-2), y = \frac{5}{4}x - 1$

20) $(0,0), y - 7x + 6 = 0$

Graphing Lines of Equations

✎ Sketch the graph of each line

1) $y = 3x - 2$

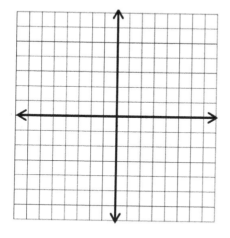

2) $y = -\frac{1}{4}x + \frac{2}{5}$

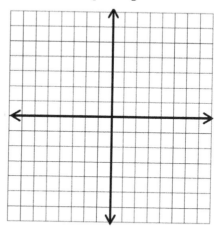

3) $4x - 2y = 6$

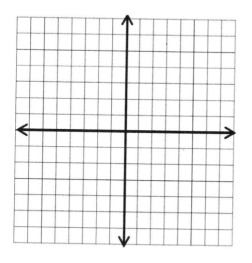

4) $-x - y = 3$

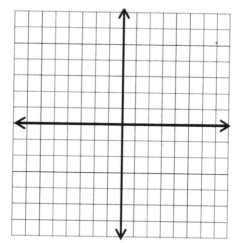

Equations of Horizontal and Vertical Lines

✏️ Sketch the graph of each line.

1) $y = 2$

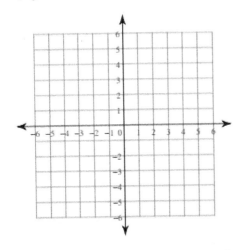

2) $y = 0$

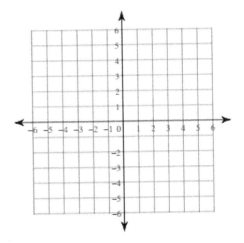

3) $x = 3$

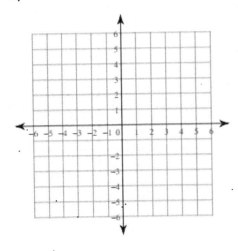

4) $x = -4$

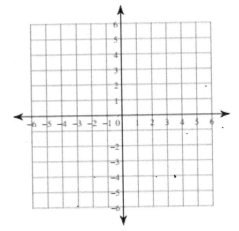

Function Notation

✍ **Write in function notation.**

1) $v = 7t$

2) $r = 2p^2 + p - 1$

3) $h = 14g + 7$

4) $y = 3x - \dfrac{2}{5}$

✍ **Evaluate each function.**

5) $w(x) = 5x + 2$, find $w(3)$

6) $h(n) = n^2 - 4$, find $h(-2)$

7) $h(x) = x^3 - 4$, find $h(-1)$

8) $h(m) = -3m^2 + 4m$, find $h(5)$

9) $f(n) = n^2 - n$, find $g(12)$

10) $g(x) = x^3 + 12x + 8$, find $g(0)$

11) $f(u) = 8u - 3$, find $g(^1/_4)$

12) $h(x) = 2x - 4$, find $h(a)$

13) $h(a) = -6a + 2$, find $h(2b)$

14) $k(a) = -2a + 1$, find $k(a - 3)$

15) $h(x) = x^3 + 2x^2 - 5$, find $h(x^2)$

16) $h(x) = x^2 + 2$, find $h(-\dfrac{x}{2})$

Adding and Subtracting Functions

Perform the indicated operation.

1) $h(t) = 3t - 2$; $g(t) = 3t + 2$
   Find $(h - g)(t)$.

2) $g(a) = -2a^2 + 1$; $f(a) = a^2 - a + 4$
   Find $(g - f)(a)$.

3) $g(x) = 3x - 4$; $h(x) = x - 7$
   Find $g(2) - h(2)$.

4) $h(3) = -2x + 1$; $g(x) = 3x - 5$
   Find $(h + g)(3)$.

5) $f(x) = 4x - 2$; $g(x) = x^2 + x$
   Find $(f - g)(-1)$.

6) $h(n) = 3n - 3$; $g(n) = n^2 - 2n + 4$
   Find $(h + g)(a)$.

7) $g(x) = -x^2 + 5 - 2x$; $f(x) = 11 + 3x$
   Find $(g - f)(x)$.

8) $h(x) = x^2 - 8$; $g(x) = -2x^2 + x$
   Find $(h + g)(t)$.

9) $g(t) = t + 7$; $f(t) = -2t^2 + t$
   Find $(g - f)(u + 1)$.

10) $k(x) = -2x + 9$; $h(x) = -x^2 + 2x - 4$
    Find $(k + h)(t - 5)$.

TSI Math Workbook

Multiplying and Dividing Functions

Perform the indicated operation.

1) $g(a) = 3a - 2;\ h(a) = 5a - 1$

   Find $(g \cdot h)(-2)$

2) $f(x) = x^3 - 2x^2;\ g(x) = 3x - 1$

   Find $(f \cdot g)(x)$

3) $g(t) = \frac{1}{2}t^2 + \frac{5}{14};\ h(t) = 21t - 46$

   Find $(h \cdot g)(-\frac{1}{7})$

4) $k(n) = n^2 - n;\ h(n) = 2n^2 + 2$

   Find $(k \cdot h)(1)$

5) $f(a) = 11a - 16;\ g(a) = 5a + 12$

   Find $(\frac{f}{g})(-2)$

6) $f(x) = x - 1;\ g(x) = x^2 - 1$

   Find $(\frac{g}{f})(x)$

7) $h(a) = -2a;\ g(a) = -a^2 - a$

   Find $(\frac{h}{g})(a)$

8) $f(t) = -a + 2;\ g(t) = a^3 - 1$

   Find $(\frac{2f}{g})(a)$

Composition of Functions

Using $f(x) = 3x - 7$, **and** $g(x) = -x + 1$, **find:**

1) $f(g(1))$

2) $f(f(0))$

3) $g(f(-5))$

Using $f(x) = -2x + 5$, **and** $g(x) = x - 4$, **find:**

4) $f(g(-3))$

5) $g(g(2))$

6) $g(f(\frac{1}{2}))$

Using $f(x) = 5x - 2a$, **and** $g(x) = x^2 - 3$, **find:**

7) $(fog)(-1) = f(g(-1))$

8) $(fof)(4)$

9) $(gof)(-1)$

Using $f(x) = -x + 5$, **and** $g(x) = x + b$, **find:**

10) $(fog)(x)$

11) $(fog)(x + 2)$

12) $(gof)(x^2)$

Answers of Worksheets – Chapter 7

Relation and Functions

1) No, $D_f = \{2, 4, 6, 8, 10\}$, $R_f = \{4, 8, 12, 16, 20\}$
2) Yes, $D_f = \{3, 0, -1, 4, 5\}$, $R_f = \{3, 0, -1, -1, 1\}$
3) Yes, $D_f = (-\infty, \infty)$, $R_f = \{-2, \infty)$
4) No, $D_f = \{2, 3, 0, 3, 1\}$, $R_f = \{-1, -2, 1, 0, 1\}$
5) No, $D_f = [-2, 2]$, $R_f = [-2, 3]$
6) Yes, $D_f = \{0, 3, 7, 5\}$, $R_f = \{2, 1, 4, 5\}$

Finding Slope

1) -2
2) -1.5
3) $-\frac{1}{3}$
4) $\frac{5}{6}$
5) $\frac{1}{7}$
6) 1
7) $-\frac{1}{2}$
8) $-\frac{1}{6}$
9) $-\frac{1}{4}$
10) Undefined
11) $-\frac{3}{4}$
12) -1

Writing Linear Equations

1) $y = -\frac{1}{2}x + 5.5$
2) $y = 3x + 7$
3) $y = \frac{1}{4}x + \frac{7}{8}$
4) $y = -\frac{1}{6}x - \frac{23}{8}$
5) $y = -7x - 7$
6) $y = -3x + 15$
7) $y = \frac{1}{2}x - \frac{1}{2}$
8) $y = -\frac{1}{3}x + \frac{4}{5}$
9) $y = 3x - 15$
10) $y = 5$
11) $y = 2x$
12) $y = x - 2$

Find the value of b

1) -4
2) 7
3) 5
4) -9

Write an equation from a graph

1) $y = 2x - 4$
2) $y = 7x + 3$
3) $y = 9x$
4) $y = 7x + 5$

Rate of change

1) 20   2) −2   3) 7

x − intercept and y−intercept

1) y − intercept = 6
   x − intercept = 4
2) y − intercept = 7
   x − intercept = −7
3) y − intercept = −15
   x − intercept = 5
4) y − intercept = 0
   x − intercept = 0
5) y − intercept = $-\frac{5}{3}$
   x − intercept = $\frac{5}{7}$
6) y − intercept = $-\frac{8}{5}$
   x − intercept = 2

Slope–intercept form

1) $y = 12x + 5$
2) $y = -5x - 15$
3) $y = -\frac{1}{2}x + 3$
4) $y = -\frac{3}{2}x - \frac{25}{4}$
5) $y = \frac{x}{2} - 4$
6) $y = \frac{7}{5}x + \frac{3}{5}$
7) $y = 2x + 4$
8) $y = \frac{3}{2}x + \frac{9}{2}$
9) $y = \frac{21}{2}x - \frac{7}{2}$
10) $y = -3x + 7$
11) $y = 3x + 8$
12) $y = -2x - 4$
13) $y = -x - 5$
14) $y = x + 11$
15) $y = \frac{5}{4}x - \frac{27}{4}$
16) $y = -\frac{1}{2}x - 2$

Point–slope form

1) $m = 3, (-2, 0)$
2) $m = \frac{2}{3}, (5, -3)$
3) 3) $m = -\frac{5}{2}, (0, -1)$
4) $m = \frac{1}{2}, (6, 6)$
5) $m = \frac{14}{10}, (-2, -2)$
6) $m = -4, (0, 7)$
7) $m = -4, (1, 30)$
8) $m = 0, (5, -15)$
9) $m = 3, (0, -5)$
10) $m = -7, (-2, 46)$
11) $y + 1 = 5(x - 2)$
12) $y - 4 = \frac{1}{2}(x + 2)$

13) $y + 8 = -x$
14) $y - b = m(x - a)$
15) $y - 3 = 5(x + 4)$
16) $y = -6(x - 2)$
17) $y - 8 = \frac{2}{3}(x + 6)$

18) $y - 12 = 0$
19) $y - 2 = \frac{1}{8}\left(x + \frac{1}{4}\right)$
20) $y = -4x$

Equation of parallel or perpendicular lines

1) $y = -\frac{4}{7}x - \frac{36}{7}$
2) $y = \frac{7}{3}x + \frac{7}{3}$
3) $y = 2x + 9$
4) $y = 3x$
5) $y = 13$
6) $y = -x + 5$
7) $y = \frac{3}{4}x + \frac{1}{4}$

8) $y = \frac{6}{5}x + \frac{21}{5}$
9) $y = -\frac{3}{5}x$
10) $y = -\frac{3}{4}x - 7$
11) $y = \frac{3}{2}x - 2$
12) $y = -3x - \frac{3}{4}$
13) $x = 3$

14) $y = -4$
15) $y = -3x - 4$
16) $y = -\frac{1}{4}x + \frac{8}{9}$
17) $y = -\frac{2}{3}x - 4$
18) $y = -x - 2$
19) $y = -\frac{4}{5}x - \frac{18}{5}$
20) $y = -\frac{1}{7}x$

Graphing Lines of Equation

1)

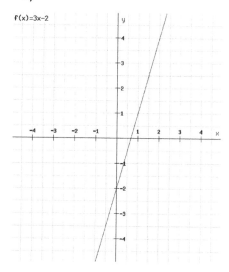

2)

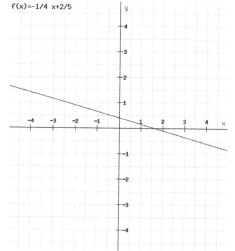

3)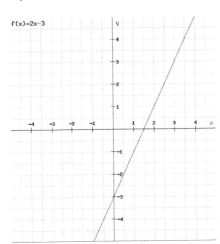

4)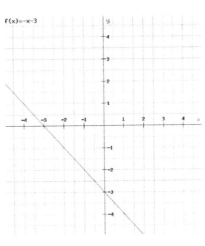

Equations of horizontal and vertical lines

1) y = 2

2) y = 0 (it is on x axes)

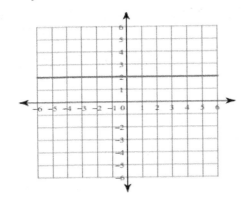

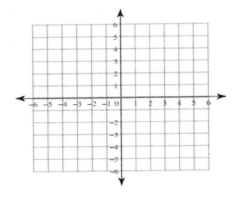

3) x = 3

4) x = − 4

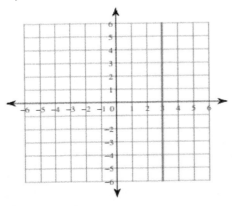

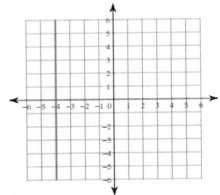

Function Notation

1) $v(t) = 7t$
2) $r(p) = 2p^2 + p - 1$
3) $h(g) = 14g + 7$
4) $f(x) = 3x - \frac{2}{5}$
5) 17
6) 0
7) -5
8) -71
9) 132
10) 8
11) -1
12) $2a - 4$
13) $-12b + 2$
14) $-2a - 7$
15) $x^6 + 2x^4 - 5$
16) $\frac{1}{4}x^2 + 2$

Adding and Subtracting Functions

1) -4
2) $-3a^2 + a - 3$
3) 7
4) -1
5) -6
6) $a^2 + a + 1$
7) $-x^2 - 5x - 6$
8) $-t^2 + t - 8$
9) $2u^2 + 4u + 9$
10) $-t^2 + 10t - 20$

Multiplying and Dividing Functions

1) 88
2) $3x^4 - 7x^3 + 2x^2$
3) $-35\frac{1}{2}$
4) 0
5) -19
6) $x + 1$
7) $\frac{2}{a+1}$
8) $\frac{-2a+4}{a^3-1}$

Composition of functions

1) -7
2) -28
3) 23
4) 19
5) -6
6) 0
7) $-10 - 2a$
8) $100 - 12a$
9) $4a^2 + 20a - 22$
10) $-x + 5 - b$
11) $-x + 3 - b$
12) $-x^2 + 5 + b$

Chapter 8

Equations and Inequalities

Topics that you'll learn in this chapter:

✓ One, Two, and Multi – Step Equations

✓ Graphing Single– Variable Inequalities

✓ One, Two, and Multi – Step Inequalities

✓ Solving Systems of Equations by Substitution and Elimination

✓ Writing and Graphing Linear Equations

✓ Finding Midpoint and Distance of Two Points

"The study of mathematics, like the Nile, begins in minuteness but ends in magnificence."
– Charles Caleb Colton

One–Step Equations

Solve each equation.

1) $x + 6 = 16$

2) $42 = (-6) + x$

3) $5x = (-50)$

4) $(-81) = (-9x)$

5) $(-6) = 4 + x$

6) $3 + x = (-4)$

7) $10x = (-110)$

8) $12 = x + 6$

9) $(-25) + x = (-20)$

10) $6x = (-36)$

11) $x - 18 = (-20)$

12) $x - 9 = (-24)$

13) $(-30) = x - 25$

14) $(-7x) = 49$

15) $(-66) = (6x)$

16) $x - 10 = 30$

17) $6x = 30$

18) $36 = (-9x)$

19) $2x = 68$

20) $25x = 500$

Two–Step Equations

Solve each equation.

1) $3(2+x) = 9$

2) $(-6)(x-3) = 42$

3) $(-10)(2x-3) = (-10)$

4) $4(1+x) = -12$

5) $14(2x+1) = 42$

6) $6(3x+2) = 42$

7) $3(7+2x) = (-60)$

8) $(-10)(2x-3) = 48$

9) $2(x+5) = 30$

10) $\dfrac{2x-6}{4} = 2$

11) $(-24) = \dfrac{x+3}{6}$

12) $110 = (-5)(x-2)$

13) $\dfrac{x}{5} - 8 = 2$

14) $-15 = 9 + \dfrac{x}{6}$

15) $\dfrac{12+x}{4} = (-10)$

16) $(-2)(6+2x) = (-100)$

17) $(-5x) + 10 = 30$

18) $\dfrac{x+6}{5} = (-5)$

19) $\dfrac{x+36}{5} = (-5)$

20) $(-8) + \dfrac{x}{4} = (-12)$

Multi–Step Equations

Solve each equation.

1) $-(3 - 2x) = 7$

2) $-18 = -(3x + 12)$

3) $5x - 15 = (-x) + 3$

4) $-225 = (-3x) - 12x$

5) $4(1 + 2x) + 2x = -16$

6) $4x - 10 = 3 + x - 5 + x$

7) $10 - 2x = (-32) - 2x + 2x$

8) $7 - 3x - 3x = 3 - 3x$

9) $26 + 11x + x = (-30) + 4x$

10) $(-3x) - 8(-1 + 5x) = 352$

11) $36 = (-6x) - 2 + 2$

12) $35 = 2x - 14 + 5x$

13) $5(1 + 5x) = -495$

14) $-40 = (-4x) - 6x$

15) $x + 5 = (-7) + 5x$

16) $5x - 8 = 8x + 4$

17) $10 = -(x - 8)$

18) $(-18) - 6x = 6(1 + 3x)$

19) $x + 2 = -3(6 + 3x)$

20) $5 = 1 - 2x + 4$

Graphing Single–Variable Inequalities

Draw a graph for each inequality.

1) $4 \geq x$

2) $x < -2$

3) $-3 < x$

4) $-x \geq 1$

5) $x > 2$

6) $-0.5 \leq x$

One–Step Inequalities

Solve each inequality and graph it.

1) $x + 3 \geq 9$

2) $x - 7 \leq 4$

3) $-4x < 2$

4) $-x + 5 > -8$

5) $x + 5 \geq -11$

6) $6x < 12$

7) $5x > -20$

Two–Step Inequalities

✏️ *Solve each inequality and graph it.*

1) $3x - 4 \leq 5$

2) $2x - 2 \leq 6$

3) $4x - 4 \leq 8$

4) $3x + 6 \geq 12$

5) $6x - 5 \geq 19$

6) $2x - 4 \leq 6$

7) $8x - 4 \leq 4$

8) $6x + 4 \leq 10$

9) $5x + 4 \leq 9$

10) $7x - 4 \leq 3$

11) $4x - 19 < 19$

12) $2x - 3 < 21$

13) $7 + 4x \geq 19$

14) $9 + 4x < 21$

15) $3 + 2x \geq 19$

16) $6 + 4x < 22$

Multi–Step Inequalities

✏️ *Solve each inequality.*

1) $\dfrac{9x}{7} - 7 < 2$

2) $\dfrac{4x + 8}{2} \leq 12$

3) $\dfrac{3x - 8}{7} > 1$

4) $-3(x - 7) > 21$

5) $4 + \dfrac{x}{3} < 7$

6) $\dfrac{2x + 6}{4} \leq 10$

Solving Systems of Equations by Substitution

Solve each system of equation by substitution.

1) $-3x + 3y = 3$
$$x + y = 3$$

2) $-10x + 2y = -6$
$$3x - 8y = 24$$

3) $y = -6$
$$15x - 10y = 75$$

4) $2y = -6x + 10$
$$10x - 8y = -6$$

5) $3x - 2y = 5$
$$3y = 3x - 3$$

6) $2x + 3y = 5$
$$3x + y = -3$$

7) $x + 10y = 6$
$$x + 5y = 1$$

8) $2x + 4y = 16$
$$x - 4, y = -1$$

Solving Systems of Equations by Elimination

✎ *Solve each system of equation by elimination.*

1) $-5x + y = -5$
$\qquad -y = -6x + 6$

2) $-6x - 2y = -2$
$\qquad 2x - 3y = 8$

3) $5x - 4y = 8$
$\qquad -6x + y = -21$

4) $10x - 4y = -24$
$\qquad -x - 20y = -18$

5) $25x + 3y = -13$
$\qquad 12x - 6y = -36$

6) $x - 8y = -7$
$\qquad 6x + 4y = 10$

7) $-6x + 16y = 4$
$\qquad 5x + y = 11$

8) $2x + 3y = 10$
$\qquad 4x + 6y = -20$

Systems of Equations Word Problems

Solve.

1) A school of 210 students went on a field trip. They took 15 vehicles, some vans and some minibuses. Find the number of vans and the number of minibuses they took if each van holds 8 students and each minibus hold 18 students.

2) The difference of two numbers is 14. Their sum is 50. Find the numbers.

3) A farmhouse shelters 15 animals, some are pigs, and some are gooses. Altogether there are 48 legs. How many of each animal are there?

4) The sum of the digits of a certain two–digit number is 9. Reversing it's increasing the number by 9. What is the number?

5) The difference of two numbers is 5. Their sum is 19. Find the numbers.

TSI Math Workbook

Graphing Linear Inequalities

✏️ *Sketch the graph of each linear inequality.*

1) $y \leq 2x - \dfrac{2}{3}$

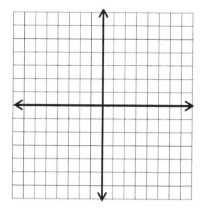

2) $-2x - 3y > \dfrac{1}{2}$

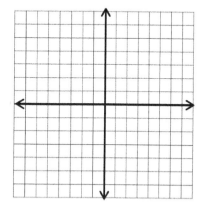

4) $-\dfrac{1}{2}x + 3y \geq -5$

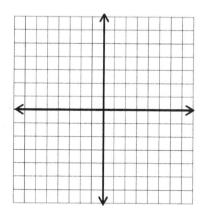

5) $3x - \dfrac{2}{7}y < 4$

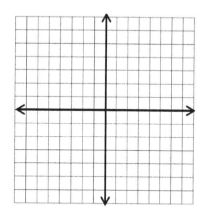

Finding Distance of Two Points

✏️ **Find the midpoint of the line segment with the given endpoints.**

1) $(1, -3), (2, -2)$

2) $(0, 2), (-1, -4)$

3) $(2, 5), (3, -5)$

4) $(1.5, 2.5), (3, 5)$

5) $(-2, 0), (0, -2)$

6) $(5, -4), (2, 5)$

7) $(1, 2), (-1, -2)$

8) $(7, 0.5), (-2, 0)$

9) $(-4, 6), (-3, -1)$

10) $(3.1, -2.7), (-1.2, 3)$

11) $(5.2, 6.3), (4, -2)$

12) $(4, 6), (-2, 4)$

✏️ **Find the distance between each pair of points.**

1) $(4, -1), (2, -1)$

2) $(5, -2), (3, 4)$

3) $(-3, -7), (-1, 2)$

4) $(7, -3), (-5, 0)$

5) $(-8, -5), (-3, -5)$

6) $(11, 1.5), (-2, -8)$

7) $(0, 6), (1, 3)$

8) $(9, 8), (-4, -3)$

9) $(2, 3), (-2, -3)$

10) $(-4, -2), (4, 2)$

11) $(-12, -15), (-7, -9)$

12) $(3, -4), (0, 0)$

Answers of Worksheets – Chapter 8

One–Step Equations

1) 10
2) 48
3) -10
4) 9
5) -10
6) -7
7) -11
8) -6
9) 5
10) -6
11) -2
12) -15
13) 5
14) 4
15) -7
16) -11
17) 40
18) 5
19) -4
20) 34
21) 20

Two–Step Equations

1) 1
2) -4
3) 2
4) -4
5) 1
6) $\dfrac{5}{3}$
7) $-\dfrac{81}{6}$
8) 0.9
9) 10
10) 7
11) -147
12) -20
13) 50
14) -144
15) -28
16) 22
17) 4
18) -31
19) -61
20) -16

Multi–Step Equations

1) 5
2) 2
3) 2
4) 15
5) -2
6) 4
7) 21
8) $\dfrac{4}{3}$
9) 7
10) -8
11) -6
12) 7
13) -20
14) 4
15) 3
16) -4
17) 1 8
18) -1
19) -2
20) 0

Graphing Single–Variable Inequalities

1) $4 \geq x$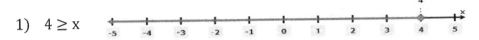

2) $x < -2$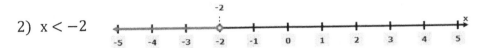

3) $-3 < x$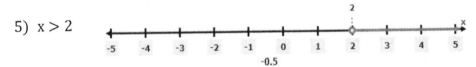

4) $-x \geq 1$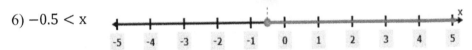

5) $x > 2$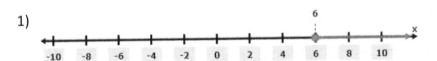

6) $-0.5 < x$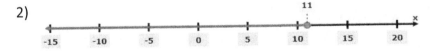

One–Step Inequalities

1)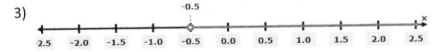

2)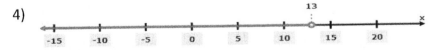

3)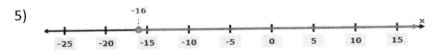

4)

5)

6)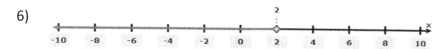

7)

Two–Step inequalities

1) $x \leq 3$
2) $x \leq 4$
3) $x \leq 3$
4) $x \geq 2$
5) $x \geq 4$
6) $x \leq 5$
7) $x \leq 1$
8) $x \leq 1$
9) $x \leq 1$
10) $x \leq 1$
11) $x < 9.5$
12) $x < 12$
13) $x \geq 3$
14) $x < 3$
15) $x \geq 8$
16) $x < 4$

Multi–Step inequalities

1) $x < 7$
2) $x \leq 4$
3) $x > 5$
4) $x < 0$
5) $x < 9$
6) $x \leq 17$

Solving Systems of Equations by Substitution

1) (0, 1)
2) (0, –3)
3) (1, –6)
4) (1, 2)
5) (3, 2)
6) (-2, 3)
7) (-4, 1)
8) $(5, \frac{3}{2})$

Solving Systems of Equations by Elimination

1) (–1, 0)
2) (1, –2)
3) (4, 3)
4) (-2, 1)
5) (–1, 4)
6) (1, 1)
7) (2, 1)
8) No solution

Systems of Equations Word Problems

1) There are 6 van and 9 minibuses.

2) 32 and 18

3) There are 9 pigs and 6 ducks.

4) 45

5) 12 and 7.

Writing Linear Equations

13) $y = -\frac{1}{2}x + 5.5$

14) $y = 3x + 7$

15) $y = \frac{1}{4}x + \frac{7}{8}$

16) $y = -\frac{1}{6}x - \frac{23}{8}$

17) $y = -7x - 7$

18) $y = -3x + 15$

19) $y = \frac{1}{2}x - \frac{1}{2}$

20) $y = -\frac{1}{3}x + \frac{4}{5}$

21) $y = 3x - 15$

22) $y = 5$

23) $y = 2x$

24) $y = x - 2$

Graphing Linear Inequalities

1)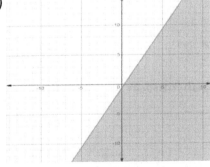

2)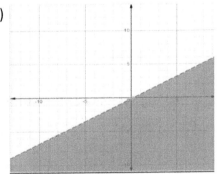

3)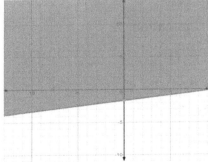

4)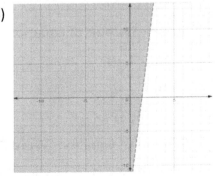

Finding Midpoint

1) $(1.5, -2.5)$
2) $(-0.5, -1)$
3) $(2.5, 0)$
4) $(2.25, 3.75)$
5) $(-2, -2)$
6) $(3.5, 0.5)$
7) $(0, 0)$
8) $(2.5, 0.25)$
9) $(-3.5, 2.5)$
10) $(0.95, 0.15)$
11) $(4.60, 2.15)$
12) $(1, 5)$

Finding Distance of Two Points

1) 1
2) 6.32
3) 9.22
4) 12.37
5) 5
6) 16.1
7) 3.16
8) 17.03
9) 7.21
10) 8.94
11) 7.81
12) 5

Chapter 9:

Polynomials

Topics that you'll learn in this chapter:

- ✓ Classifying and Simplifying Polynomials
- ✓ Writing Polynomials in Standard Form
- ✓ Adding and Subtracting Polynomials
- ✓ Multiplying and Dividing Monomials
- ✓ Multiplying a Polynomial and a Monomial
- ✓ Multiplying Binomials
- ✓ Factoring Trinomials
- ✓ Operations with Polynomials

Mathematics – the unshaken Foundation of Sciences, and the plentiful Fountain of Advantage to human affairs. – Isaac Barrow

Classifying Polynomials

✎ Name each polynomial by degree and number of terms.

1) $x + 4$

2) -8

3) $-5x^4$

4) $9x^2 - 8x^3$

5) $2x - 1$

6) $8x^5$

7) $9x^2 - x$

✎ Write each polynomial in standard form

1) $x^2 - 4x^3$

2) $x^2 + x - x3$

3) $12 - 7x + 9x^4$

4) $x^2 + 12x - 8x3$

5) $x(x + 2) - (x + 2)$

6) $x^2 + x + 13 - 8x^2 - 4x$

7) $10x^5 + x^3 - 3x^5 - 4x^3$

8) $x(x + 6 - 8x^2)$

9) $x(x^5 + 2x^3)$

10) $(x + 4)(x + 2)$

11) $(x + 3)2$

12) $(x - 5)(2x + 3)$

13) $x(1 + 3x^2 + 2x)$

14) $x(2 - x + 2x^3)$

Simplifying Polynomials

✍ Simplify each expression.

1) $5 - 3x^2 + 7x^2 - 2x\ 3 + 6$

2) $23x\ 5 - 3x\ 3 + 7x^2 - 23x5$

3) $(-2)(x^6 + 9) - 6(10 + x^6)$

4) $3(2x^2 + 4x^2 + 3x^3) - 9x^3 + 17$

5) $3 - 6x^2 + 8x^2 - 13x^3 + 26$

6) $x^2 - 2x + 3x^3 + 16x - 20x$

7) $(x - 6)(3x - 5)$

8) $(12x + y)^2$

9) $(12x^3 + 28x^2 + 10x + 4) \div (x + 2)$

10) $(2x + 12x^2 - 2) \div (2x + 1)$

11) $(x^3 - 1) + (4x^3 - 3x^3)$

12) $(x - 2)(x + 3)$

13) $(2x + 6)(2x - 6)$

14) $(x^2 - 3x) + (5x - 5 - 8x^2)$

Adding and Subtracting Polynomials

1) $(4x^3 + 8) - (9 + 5x^3)$

2) $(x^3 + 8) + (x^3 - 8)$

3) $(2x^2 + 5x^3) - (5x^3 + 9)$

4) $(5x^2 - 2x) + (3x - 6x^2)$

5) $(12x - 7x^3) - (4x^3 + 4x)$

6) $(2x^3 - x^2) - (3x^2 - 4x^3)$

7) $(x^2 - 8) + (8x^2 - 3x^3)$

8) $(x^3 + x4) - (x4 + 5x^3)$

9) $(-10x^4 + 12x^5 + x^3) + (14x^3 + 10x^5 + 16x^4)$

10) $(12x^2 - 6x^5 - 2x) + (-10x^2 - 11x^5 + 9x)$

11) $(35 + 8x^5 - 4x^2) + (7x4 + 2x^5) - (27 - 4x^4)$

12) $(4x^5 - 3x^3 - 3x) + (3x + 10x^4 - 12) + (2x^2 + x^3 + 10)$

Multiplying Monomials

1) $4xy^2z \times 3z^2$

2) $6xy \times 2x^2y$

3) $6pq^3 \times (-3p^4q)$

4) $6s^4t^2 \times st^5$

5) $12p^3 \times (-4p^4)$

6) $-4p^2q^3r \times 4pq^2r^3$

7) $(-4) \times (-24a^6b)$

8) $2u^4v^2 \times (-10u^2v^3)$

9) $5u^3 \times (-3u)$

10) $-8xy^2 \times 4x^2y$

11) $24y^2z^3 \times (-y^2z)$

12) $10a^2bc^2 \times 3abc^2$

Multiply Binomials

1) $(x - 2)(5x + 2)$
2) $(3x - 2)(x + 5)$
3) $(x + 2)(x + 8)$
4) $(x^2 + 3)(x^2 - 3)$
5) $(x - 3)(x + 6)$
6) $(x - 6)(2x + 6)$
7) $(x - 4)(3x - 3)$
8) $(x - 5)(x - 4)$
9) $(x + 5)(2x + 5)$
10) $(x - 6)(3x + 6)$
11) $(x - 8)(x + 8)$
12) $(x - 4)(4x + 8)$
13) $(2x - 6)(2x + 6)$
14) $(x + 7)(x - 2)$
15) $(x - 7)(x + 7)$
16) $(4x + 4)(4x - 3)$

Multiply and Divide Monomials

1) $(8x^4y^6)(4x^3y^4)$
2) $\dfrac{60x^5y^8}{40x^7y^{11}}$
3) $(14x^4)(4x^9)$
4) $\dfrac{60x^{12}y^9}{20x^6y^7}$
5) $(-2x^{-4}y^2)^5$
6) $\dfrac{85x^{18}y^7}{5x^9y^2}$
7) $(12x^2y^9)(6x^9y^{12})$
8) $\dfrac{200x^3y^8}{20x^3y^7}$
9) $(3x^{-5}y^4)^{-2}$
10) $\dfrac{-18x^{17}y^{13}}{3x^6y^9}$
11) $(-5x^{-3}y^{-1})(-4x^{-4}y^3)$
12) $\dfrac{-81x^8y^{10}}{9x^3y^7}$

Multiply a Polynomial and a Monomial

1) $4(3x - 4y)$

2) $9x(3x + 5y)$

3) $8x(8x - 5)$

4) $12x(3x + 9)$

5) $12x(2x - 2y)$

6) $3x(5x - 6y)$

7) $x(2x^2 - 3x + 8)$

8) $12x(2x + 4y)$

9) $30(2x^2 - 8x - 5)$

10) $6x^3(3x^2 - x + 1)$

11) $8x^2(4x^2 - 5xy + y^2)$

12) $x^2(3x^2 - 5x + 10)$

13) $2x^3(x^2 + 6x - 2)$

14) $4x(3x^2 - 4xy + 2y^2)$

Factor Trinomials

1) $x^2 - 6x + 8$

2) $x^2 - 5x - 14$

3) $x^2 - 10x - 24$

4) $2x^2 + 3x - 9$

5) $x^2 - 16x + 48$

6) $x^2 + 3x - 18$

7) $3x^2 + 7x + 2$

8) $x^2 - 3x - 10$

9) $8x^2 + 22x - 6$

10) $x^2 + 22x + 121$

11) $64x^2 + 16xy + 4y^2$

12) $6x^2 - 20x + 16$

13) $x^2 - 12x + 36$

14) $25x^2 + 20x + 4$

Operations with Polynomials

1) $2x^2(4x-3)$

2) $4x^2(6x-3)$

3) $-5(5x-3)$

4) $4x^3(-4x+6)$

5) $7(7x+2)$

6) $9(3x+7)$

7) $4(7x+1)$

8) $-6x^4(x-4)$

9) $8(x^2-2x+3)$

10) $2(4x^2-2x+1)$

11) $2(4x^2+3x-2)$

12) $7x(2x^2+3x+8)$

13) $(8x+1)(2x-1)$

14) $(x+5)(3x-5)$

15) $(6x-4)(3x-6)$

16) $(x-4)(3x+6)$

Answers of Worksheets – Chapter 9

Classifying Polynomials

1) Linear monomial
2) Constant monomial
3) Quantic monomial
4) cubic binomial
5) linear binomial
6) Quantic monomial
7) Quadratic binomial

Writing Polynomials in Standard Form

1) $-4x^3 + x^2$
2) $-x^3 + x^2 + x$
3) $9x^4 - 7x + 12$
4) $-8x^3 + x^2 + 12x$
5) $x^2 + x - 2$
6) $-7x^2 - 3x + 13$
7) $7x^5 - 3x^3$
8) $-8x^3 + x^2 + 6x$
9) $x^6 + 2x^4$
10) $x^2 + 6x + 8$
11) $x^2 + 6x + 9$
12) $2x^2 - 7x - 15$
13) $3x^3 + 2x^2 + x$
14) $2x^4 - x^2 + 2$

Simplifying Polynomials

1) $-2x^3 + 4x^2 + 11$
2) $-3x^3 + 7x^2$
3) $-8x^6 - 78$
4) $18x^2 + 17$
5) $-13x^3 + 2x^2 + 29$
6) $3x^3 + x^2 - 6x$
7) $3x^2 - 23x + 30$
8) $144x^2 + 24xy + y^2$
9) $12x^2 + 4x + 2$
10) $6x - 1$
11) $2x^3 - 1$
12) $x^2 - x - 6$
13) $4x^2 - 36$
14) $-8x^2 - +2x - 5$

TSI Math Workbook

Adding and Subtracting Polynomials

1) $-x^3 - 1$
2) $2x^3$
3) $2x^2 - 9$
4) $-x^2 + x$
5) $-11x^3 + 8x$
6) $6x^3 - 4x^2$
7) $-3x^3 + 9x^2 - 8$
8) $-4x^3$
9) $22x^5 + 6x^4 + 15x^3$
10) $5x^5 + 23x^2 - 11x$
11) $7x^5 + 11x^4 - 4x^2 + 8$
12) $4x^5 + 10x^4 - 2x^3 + 2x^2 - 2$

Multiply Monomials

1) $12xy^2z^3$
2) $12x^3y^2$
3) $-18p^5q^4$
4) $6s^5t^7$
5) $-48p^7$
6) $-16p^3q^5r^4$
7) $96a^{10}b$
8) $-20u^6v^5$
9) $-15u^4$
10) $-32x^3y^3$
11) $-24y^4z^4$
12) $30a^3b^2c^4$

Multiply and Divide Monomials

1) $32x^7y^{10}$
2) $1.5x^{-2}y^{-3}$
3) $56x^{13}$
4) $3x^6y^2$
5) $-32x^{-15}y^{10}$
6) $17x^9y^5$
7) $72x^{11}y^{21}$
8) $10y$
9) $\frac{1}{9}x^{10}y^{-8}$
10) $-6x^{11}y^4$
11) $(20x^{-7}y^2)$
12) $-9x^5y^3$

Multiply a Polynomial and a Monomial

1) $12x - 16y$
2) $18x^2 + 45xy$
3) $64x^2 - 40x$
4) $36x^2 + 108x$
5) $24x^2 - 24xy$
6) $15x^2 - 18xy$
7) $2x^3 - 3x^2 + 8x$
8) $24x^2 + 48xy$
9) $60x^2 - 240x - 150$
10) $18x^5 - 6x^4 + 6x^3$
11) $32x^4 - 40x^3y + 8y^2x^2$
12) $3x^4 - 5x^3 + 10x^2$
13) $42x^5 + 12x^4 - 4x^3$
14) $12x^3 - 16x^2y + 8xy^2$

Multiplying Binomials

1) $5x^2 - 8x - 4$
2) $2x^2 + 9x - 35$

3) $x^2 + 10x + 16$
4) $x^4 - 9$
5) $x^2 + 3x - 18$
6) $2x^2 - 6x - 36$
7) $3x^2 - 15x - 12$
8) $x^2 - 9x + 20$
9) $2x^2 + 15x + 25$

10) $3x^2 - 13x - 36$
11) $x^2 - 64$
12) $3x^2 - 13x - 32$
13) $4x^2 - 36$
14) $x^2 + 5x - 14$
15) $x^2 - 49$
16) $16x^2 + 4x - 12$

Factoring Trinomials

1) $(x - 4)(x - 2)$
2) $(x + 2)(x - 7)$
3) $(x + 2)(x - 12)$
4) $(x + 3)(2x - 3)$
5) $(x - 14)(x - 2)$
6) $(x - 3)(x + 6)$
7) $(3x + 1)(x + 2)$

8) $(x - 5)(x + 2)$
9) $(4x - 1)(2x + 6)$
10) $(x + 11)(x + 11)$
11) $(8x + 2y)(8x + 2y)$
12) $(2x - 4)(3x - 4)$
13) $(x - 6)(x - 6)$
14) $(5x + 2)(5x + 2)$

Operations with Polynomials

1) $8x^3 - 6x^2$
2) $24x^3 - 12x^2$
3) $-25x + 15$
4) $-16x^4 + 24x^3$
5) $49x + 14$
6) $18x + 63$
7) $28x + 4$
8) $-6x^5 + 24x^4$

9) $8x^2 - 16x + 24$
10) $8x^2 - 4x + 2$
11) $8x^2 + 6x - 4$
12) $14x^3 + 21x^2 + 56x$
13) $16x^2 - 6x - 1$
14) $3x^2 + 10x - 25$
15) $18x^2 - 48x + 24$
16) $3x^2 - 6x - 24$

Chapter 10:
Quadratic Functions

Topics that you'll learn in this chapter:

- ✓ Graphing Quadratic Functions
- ✓ Solving Quadratic Equations
- ✓ Use the Quadratic Formula and the Discriminant
- ✓ Solve Quadratic Inequalities
- ✓ Adding, Subtracting and Multiplications Matrices
- ✓ Finding Determinants of a Matrix
- ✓ Finding Inverse of a Matrix
- ✓ Matrix Equations

"It's fine to work on any problem, so long as it generates interesting mathematics along the way – even if you don't solve it at the end of the day." – Andrew Wiles

Graphing Quadratic Functions

✏️ *Sketch the graph of each function. Identify the vertex and axis of symmetry.*

1) $y = 2(x + 2)^2 - 3$

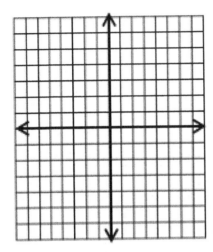

2) $y = -2(x + 2)^2 + 4$

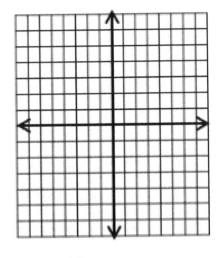

3) $x = -y^2 + 3y + 4$

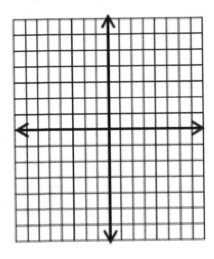

4) $y = (y + 1)^2 - 2$

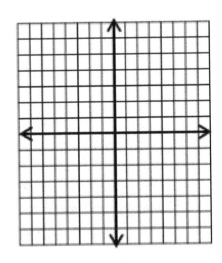

Solving Quadratic Equations

✍ *Solve each equation by factoring or by using the quadratic formula.*

1) $x^2 + x - 20 = 2x$

2) $x^2 + 8x = -15$

3) $7x^2 - 14x = -7$

4) $6x^2 - 18x - 18 = 6$

5) $2x^2 + 6x - 24 = 12$

6) $2x^2 - 22x + 38 = -10$

7) $(2x + 5)(4x + 3) = 0$

8) $(x + 2)(x - 7) = 0$

9) $(x + 3)(x + 5) = 0$

10) $(5x + 7)(x + 4) = 0$

11) $-4x^2 - 8x - 3 = -3 - 5x^2$

12) $10x^2 = 27x - 18$

13) $7x^2 - 6x + 3 = 3$

14) $x^2 = 2x$

15) $2x^2 - 14 = -3x$

16) $10x^2 - 26x = -12$

17) $15x^2 + 80 = -80x$

18) $x^2 + 15x = -56$

Use the Quadratic Formula and the Discriminant

✏️ *Find the value of the discriminant of each quadratic equation.*

1) $2x^2 + 5x - 4 = 0$

2) $x^2 + 5x + 2 = 0$

3) $5x^2 + x - 2 = 0$

4) $-4x^2 - 4x + 5 = 0$

5) $-2x^2 - x - 1 = 0$

6) $6x^2 - 2x - 3 = 0$

7) $x(x - 1)$

8) $8x^2 - 9x = 0$

9) $3x^2 - 5x + 1 = 0$

10) $5x^2 + 6x + 4 = 0$

✏️ *Find the discriminant of each quadratic equation then state the number of real and imaginary solution.*

11) $8x^2 - 6x + 3 = 5x^2$

12) $-4x^2 - 4x = 6$

13) $-x^2 - 9 = 6x$

14) $-9x^2 = -8x + 8$

15) $4x^2 = 8x - 4$

16) $9x^2 + 6x + 6 = 5$

17) $9x^2 - 3x - 8 = -10$

18) $-2x^2 - 8x - 14 = -6$

Solve Quadratic Inequalities

🖎 *Solve each quadratic inequality.*

1) $-x^2 - 5x + 6 > 0$

2) $x^2 - 5x - 6 < 0$

3) $x^2 + 4x - 5 > 0$

4) $x^2 - 2x - 3 \geq 0$

5) $x^2 - 1 < 0$

6) $17x^2 + 15x - 2 \geq 0$

7) $4x^2 + 20x - 11 < 0$

8) $12x^2 + 10x - 12 > 0$

9) $18x^2 + 23x + 5 \leq 0$

10) $-9x^2 + 29x - 6 \geq 0$

11) $-8x^2 + 6x - 1 \leq 0$

12) $5x^2 - 15x + 10 < 0$

13) $3x^2 - 5x \geq 4x^2 + 6$

14) $x^2 > 5x + 6$

15) $3x^2 + 7x \leq 5x^2 + 3x - 6$

16) $4x^2 - 12 > 3x^2 + x$

17) $3x^2 - 5x \geq 4x^2 + 6$

18) $2x^2 + 2x - 8 > x^2$

TSI Math Workbook

Adding and Subtracting Matrices

✏️ *Simplify.*

1) $\begin{vmatrix} -6 & 3 & -4 \end{vmatrix} + \begin{vmatrix} 2 & -3 & -1 \end{vmatrix}$

2) $\begin{vmatrix} 2 & 3 \\ -1 & -2 \\ -4 & -1 \end{vmatrix} + \begin{vmatrix} 0 & -1 \\ 1 & 0 \\ 2 & 5 \end{vmatrix}$

3) $\begin{vmatrix} -2 & 0 & -1 \\ 4 & -2 & 0 \end{vmatrix} - \begin{vmatrix} 6 & -2 & -1 \\ 1 & 4 & -3 \end{vmatrix}$

4) $\begin{vmatrix} 5 & 2 \end{vmatrix} + \begin{vmatrix} -2 & -7 \end{vmatrix}$

5) $\begin{vmatrix} 1 \\ 4 \end{vmatrix} + \begin{vmatrix} 3 \\ 6 \end{vmatrix}$

6) $\begin{vmatrix} -r+t \\ -r \\ 3s \end{vmatrix} + \begin{vmatrix} r \\ -2t \\ -2r+2 \end{vmatrix}$

7) $\begin{vmatrix} z-2 \\ -4 \\ -1-5z \\ 2y \end{vmatrix} + \begin{vmatrix} -y \\ z \\ 5+z \\ 4z \end{vmatrix}$

8) $\begin{vmatrix} -4n & n+m \\ -2n & -4m \end{vmatrix} + \begin{vmatrix} 4 & -2 \\ m & 0 \end{vmatrix}$

9) $\begin{vmatrix} 2 & 3 \\ -6 & 5 \end{vmatrix} - \begin{vmatrix} 0 & -3 \\ 1 & 10 \end{vmatrix}$

10) $\begin{vmatrix} 1 & -5 & 9 \\ 4 & -3 & 11 \\ -6 & 3 & -15 \end{vmatrix} + \begin{vmatrix} 3 & 4 & -5 \\ 5 & 2 & 0 \\ 4 & -5 & 1 \end{vmatrix}$

Matrix Multiplication

Simplify.

1) $\begin{vmatrix} -1 & -1 \\ -1 & 2 \end{vmatrix} \times \begin{vmatrix} -2 & -3 \\ 3 & 2 \end{vmatrix}$

2) $\begin{vmatrix} 0 & 3 \\ -3 & 1 \\ -5 & 1 \end{vmatrix} \times \begin{vmatrix} -2 & 2 \\ -2 & -4 \end{vmatrix}$

3) $\begin{vmatrix} 4 & 2 & 5 \\ 2 & 5 & 1 \end{vmatrix} \times \begin{vmatrix} 4 & 6 & -5 \\ 5 & -1 & 0 \end{vmatrix}$

4) $\begin{vmatrix} -4 \\ 0 \\ 2 \end{vmatrix} \times |2 \quad -1|$

5) $\begin{vmatrix} 2 & -1 \\ 0 & 6 \\ -2 & -2 \end{vmatrix} \times \begin{vmatrix} -1 & 6 \\ 5 & 4 \end{vmatrix}$

6) $\begin{vmatrix} -1 & -3 \\ -2 & 3 \\ 3 & 0 \\ 4 & -2 \end{vmatrix} \times \begin{vmatrix} 1 & -2 & 1 \\ -1 & 0 & -3 \end{vmatrix}$

7) $\begin{vmatrix} -2 & -y \\ -x & -2 \end{vmatrix} \cdot \begin{vmatrix} -x & 0 \\ y & -2 \end{vmatrix}$

8) $|1 \quad -4v| \cdot \begin{vmatrix} -2u & -v \\ 0 & 3 \end{vmatrix}$

9) $\begin{vmatrix} -1 & 1 & -1 \\ 0 & 2 & -1 \\ 2 & -5 & 1 \\ -5 & 6 & 0 \end{vmatrix} \cdot \begin{vmatrix} 2 & 1 \\ 1 & -2 \\ 3 & 0 \end{vmatrix}$

10) $\begin{vmatrix} 5 & 3 & 5 \\ 1 & 5 & 0 \end{vmatrix} \cdot \begin{vmatrix} -4 & 2 \\ -3 & 4 \\ 3 & -5 \end{vmatrix}$

11) $\begin{vmatrix} -1 & 5 \\ -2 & 1 \end{vmatrix} \cdot \begin{vmatrix} 6 & -2 \\ 1 & 0 \end{vmatrix}$

12) $\begin{vmatrix} 0 & 2 \\ -2 & -5 \end{vmatrix} \cdot \begin{vmatrix} 2 & -1 \\ 3 & 0 \end{vmatrix}$

Finding Determinants of a Matrix

✏️ *Evaluate the determinant of each matrix.*

1) $\begin{vmatrix} 0 & -3 \\ -6 & -2 \end{vmatrix}$

2) $\begin{vmatrix} 0 & 3 \\ 2 & 6 \end{vmatrix}$

3) $\begin{vmatrix} -1 & 1 \\ -1 & 2 \end{vmatrix}$

4) $\begin{vmatrix} -2 & -9 \\ -1 & -10 \end{vmatrix}$

5) $\begin{vmatrix} -1 & 6 \\ 5 & 0 \end{vmatrix}$

6) $\begin{vmatrix} 8 & -6 \\ 0 & 9 \end{vmatrix}$

7) $\begin{vmatrix} 2 & -2 \\ 5 & -4 \end{vmatrix}$

8) $\begin{vmatrix} 2 & 6 \\ 3 & 9 \end{vmatrix}$

9) $\begin{vmatrix} 0 & 2 \\ -6 & 0 \end{vmatrix}$

10) $\begin{vmatrix} 0 & 4 \\ 4 & 5 \end{vmatrix}$

11) $\begin{vmatrix} 2 & -3 & 1 \\ 2 & 0 & -1 \\ 1 & 4 & 5 \end{vmatrix}$

12) $\begin{vmatrix} -5 & 0 & -1 \\ 1 & 2 & -1 \\ -3 & 4 & 1 \end{vmatrix}$

13) $\begin{vmatrix} 6 & 1 & 1 \\ 4 & -2 & 5 \\ 2 & 8 & 7 \end{vmatrix}$

14) $\begin{vmatrix} 3 & -5 & 3 \\ 2 & 1 & -1 \\ 1 & 0 & 4 \end{vmatrix}$

15) $\begin{vmatrix} 1 & 3 & 2 \\ 3 & -1 & -3 \\ 2 & 3 & 1 \end{vmatrix}$

Finding Inverse of a Matrix

Find the inverse of each matrix.

1) $\begin{vmatrix} 4 & 7 \\ 2 & 6 \end{vmatrix}$

2) $\begin{vmatrix} 2 & 1 \\ 3 & 2 \end{vmatrix}$

3) $\begin{vmatrix} 4 & 3 \\ 2 & 1 \end{vmatrix}$

4) $\begin{vmatrix} -9 & 6 \\ 4 & 3 \end{vmatrix}$

5) $\begin{vmatrix} -3 & 2 \\ 1 & 3 \end{vmatrix}$

6) $\begin{vmatrix} 2 & 4 \\ 5 & 2 \end{vmatrix}$

7) $\begin{vmatrix} 0 & 7 \\ 3 & 2 \end{vmatrix}$

8) $\begin{vmatrix} -6 & -11 \\ 2 & 7 \end{vmatrix}$

9) $\begin{vmatrix} -1 & 8 \\ -1 & 8 \end{vmatrix}$

10) $\begin{vmatrix} -1 & 1 \\ 6 & 3 \end{vmatrix}$

11) $\begin{vmatrix} 11 & 5 \\ 2 & 1 \end{vmatrix}$

12) $\begin{vmatrix} 0 & 2 \\ 1 & 9 \end{vmatrix}$

13) $\begin{vmatrix} 0 & 0 \\ -6 & 3 \end{vmatrix}$

14) $\begin{vmatrix} 3 & 4 \\ 6 & 8 \end{vmatrix}$

Matrix Equations

✎ *Solve each equation.*

1) $\begin{vmatrix} -1 & 2 \\ -2 & 5 \end{vmatrix} z = \begin{vmatrix} 6 \\ 20 \end{vmatrix}$

2) $2x = \begin{vmatrix} 12 & -12 \\ 24 & -8 \end{vmatrix}$

3) $\begin{vmatrix} -3 & 2 \\ -11 & 6 \end{vmatrix} = \begin{vmatrix} 2 & 8 \\ 5 & 9 \end{vmatrix} - x$

4) $Y - \begin{vmatrix} -2 \\ -4 \\ 10 \\ 10 \end{vmatrix} = \begin{vmatrix} -6 \\ 6 \\ -16 \\ 0 \end{vmatrix}$

5) $\begin{vmatrix} -1 & -3 \\ 0 & -4 \end{vmatrix} C = \begin{vmatrix} 10 \\ 8 \end{vmatrix}$

6) $\begin{vmatrix} -1 & -3 \\ 2 & 8 \end{vmatrix} B = \begin{vmatrix} -8 & -2 & 8 \\ 22 & 0 & -20 \end{vmatrix}$

7) $\begin{vmatrix} -1 & 1 \\ 5 & -2 \end{vmatrix} C = \begin{vmatrix} 1 \\ -11 \end{vmatrix}$

8) $\begin{vmatrix} 1 & 2 \\ 3 & 4 \end{vmatrix} C = \begin{vmatrix} 11 \\ 21 \end{vmatrix}$

9) $\begin{vmatrix} 0 & -4 \\ 3 & 3 \end{vmatrix} Z = \begin{vmatrix} 20 \\ 6 \end{vmatrix}$

10) $\begin{vmatrix} -10 \\ 15 \\ -20 \end{vmatrix} = 5B$

11) $\begin{vmatrix} -10 \\ 4 \\ 3 \end{vmatrix} = y - \begin{vmatrix} 7 \\ -5 \\ -11 \end{vmatrix}$

12) $-4b - \begin{vmatrix} 5 \\ 2 \\ -6 \end{vmatrix} = \begin{vmatrix} -33 \\ -2 \\ -22 \end{vmatrix}$

Answers of Worksheets – Chapter 10

Graphing quadratic functions

1)
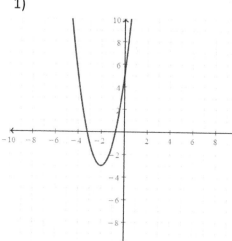

2)
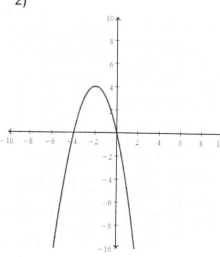

3)
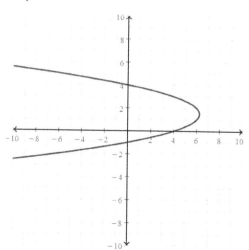

4)
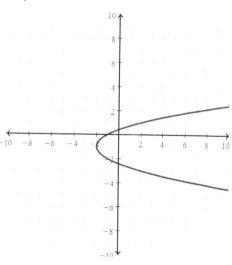

Solving quadratic equations

1) $\{5, -4\}$

2) $\{-5, -3\}$

3) $\{1\}$

4) $\{4, -1\}$

5) $\{3, -6\}$

6) $\{3, 8\}$

7) $\{-\frac{5}{2}, -\frac{3}{4}\}$

8) $\{-2, 7\}$

9) $\{-3, -5\}$

10) $\{-\frac{7}{5}, -4\}$

11) $\{8, 0\}$

TSI Math Workbook

12) $\{\frac{6}{5}, \frac{3}{2}\}$

13) $\{\frac{6}{7}, 0\}$

14) $\{2, 0\}$

15) $\{-\frac{7}{2}, 2\}$

16) $\{\frac{3}{5}, 2\}$

17) $\{-\frac{4}{3}, -4\}$

18) $\{-8, -7\}$

Use the quadratic formula and the discriminant

1) 57
2) 17
3) 41
4) 96

5) −7
6) 76
7) 21
8) 81

9) 13
10) −44

11) 0, one real solution
12) −80, no solution
13) 0, one real solution
14) −224, no solution

15) 0, one real solution
16) 0, one real solution
17) −63, solution
18) 0, one real solution

Solve quadratic inequalities

1) $-6 < x < 1$

2) $-1 < x < 6$

3) $x < -5$ or $x > 1$

4) $x \leq -1$ or $x \geq 3$

5) $-1 < x < 1$

6) $x \leq -1$ or $x \geq \frac{2}{17}$

7) $-\frac{11}{2} < x < \frac{1}{2}$

8) $x < -\frac{3}{2}$ or $x > \frac{2}{3}$

9) $-1 \leq x \leq -\frac{5}{18}$

10) $\frac{2}{9} \leq x \leq 3$

11) $x \leq \frac{1}{4}$ or $x \geq \frac{1}{2}$

12) $1 < x < 2$

13) $-3 \leq x \leq -2$

14) $x < -1$ or $x > 6$

15) $x \leq -1$ or $x \geq 3$

16) $x < -3$ or $x > 4$

17) $-3 \leq x \leq -2$

18) $x < -4$ or $x > 2$

Adding and Subtracting Matrices

1) $|-4 \quad 0 \quad -5|$

2) $\begin{vmatrix} 2 & 2 \\ 0 & -2 \\ -2 & 4 \end{vmatrix}$

3) $\begin{vmatrix} -9 & 2 & 0 \\ 3 & -6 & 3 \end{vmatrix}$

4) $|3 \quad -5|$

5) $\begin{vmatrix} 4 \\ 10 \end{vmatrix}$

TSI Math Workbook

6) $\begin{vmatrix} t \\ -r - 2t \\ 3s - 2r + 2 \end{vmatrix}$

7) $\begin{vmatrix} z - 2 - y \\ -4 + z \\ 4 - 4z \\ 2y + 4z \end{vmatrix}$

8) $\begin{vmatrix} -4n + 4 & n + m - 2 \\ -2n + m & -4m \end{vmatrix}$

9) $\begin{vmatrix} 2 & 6 \\ -7 & -5 \end{vmatrix}$

10) $\begin{vmatrix} 4 & -1 & 4 \\ 9 & -1 & 11 \\ -2 & -2 & -14 \end{vmatrix}$

Matrix Multiplication

1) $\begin{vmatrix} -1 & 1 \\ 8 & 7 \end{vmatrix}$

2) $\begin{vmatrix} -6 & -12 \\ 4 & -10 \\ 8 & -14 \end{vmatrix}$

3) Undefined

4) $\begin{vmatrix} -8 & 4 \\ 0 & 0 \\ 4 & -2 \end{vmatrix}$

5) $\begin{vmatrix} -7 & 8 \\ 30 & 24 \\ -8 & -20 \end{vmatrix}$

6) $\begin{vmatrix} 2 & 2 & 10 \\ -5 & 4 & -11 \\ 3 & -6 & 3 \\ 6 & -8 & 11 \end{vmatrix}$

7) $\begin{vmatrix} 2x - y^2 & 2y \\ x^2 - 2y & 4 \end{vmatrix}$

8) $\begin{vmatrix} -2u & -13v \end{vmatrix}$

9) $\begin{vmatrix} -7 & -3 \\ -1 & -4 \\ 2 & 12 \\ 4 & -17 \end{vmatrix}$

10) $\begin{vmatrix} -14 & -3 \\ -19 & 22 \end{vmatrix}$

11) $\begin{vmatrix} -1 & 2 \\ -11 & 4 \end{vmatrix}$

12) $\begin{vmatrix} 6 & 0 \\ -19 & 2 \end{vmatrix}$

Finding Determinants of a Matrix

1) −18

2) -6

3) −1

4) 11

5) −30

6) 72

7) 2

8) 0

9) −12

10) −16

11) 49

12) -40

13) −306

14) 54

15) -15

TSI Math Workbook

Finding Inverse of a Matrix

1) $\begin{vmatrix} \frac{6}{10} & \frac{-7}{10} \\ \frac{-1}{5} & \frac{2}{5} \end{vmatrix}$

2) $\begin{vmatrix} 2 & -1 \\ -3 & 2 \end{vmatrix}$

3) $\begin{vmatrix} -\frac{1}{2} & \frac{3}{2} \\ 1 & -2 \end{vmatrix}$

4) $\begin{vmatrix} -\frac{3}{51} & \frac{6}{51} \\ \frac{4}{51} & \frac{9}{51} \end{vmatrix}$

5) $\begin{vmatrix} -\frac{3}{11} & \frac{2}{11} \\ \frac{1}{11} & \frac{3}{11} \end{vmatrix}$

6) $\begin{vmatrix} -\frac{2}{16} & \frac{4}{16} \\ \frac{5}{16} & -\frac{2}{16} \end{vmatrix}$

7) $\begin{vmatrix} -\frac{2}{21} & \frac{7}{21} \\ \frac{3}{21} & 0 \end{vmatrix}$

8) $\begin{vmatrix} -\frac{7}{20} & -\frac{11}{20} \\ \frac{2}{20} & \frac{6}{20} \end{vmatrix}$

9) No inverse exists

10) $\begin{vmatrix} -\frac{3}{9} & \frac{1}{9} \\ \frac{6}{9} & \frac{1}{9} \end{vmatrix}$

11) $\begin{vmatrix} 1 & -5 \\ -2 & 11 \end{vmatrix}$

12) $\begin{vmatrix} -\frac{9}{2} & 1 \\ \frac{1}{2} & 0 \end{vmatrix}$

13) No inverse exists

14) No inverse exists

Matrix Equations

1) $\begin{vmatrix} 10 \\ 8 \end{vmatrix}$

2) $\begin{vmatrix} 6 & -6 \\ 12 & -4 \end{vmatrix}$

3) $\begin{vmatrix} 5 & 6 \\ 11 & 3 \end{vmatrix}$

4) $\begin{vmatrix} -4 \\ 2 \\ -6 \\ 10 \end{vmatrix}$

5) $\begin{vmatrix} 4 \\ -2 \end{vmatrix}$

6) $\begin{vmatrix} -1 & 8 & -2 \\ 3 & -2 & -2 \end{vmatrix}$

7) $\begin{vmatrix} -3 \\ -2 \end{vmatrix}$

8) $\begin{vmatrix} -1 \\ 6 \end{vmatrix}$

9) $\begin{vmatrix} -5 \\ -3 \end{vmatrix}$

10) $\begin{vmatrix} -2 \\ 3 \\ -4 \end{vmatrix}$

11) $\begin{vmatrix} -3 \\ -1 \\ -8 \end{vmatrix}$

12) $\begin{vmatrix} 7 \\ 0 \\ 7 \end{vmatrix}$

Chapter 11: Trigonometric Functions

Topics that you'll learn in this chapter:

- ✓ Trig ratios of General Angles
- ✓ Sketch Each Angle in Standard Position
- ✓ Finding Co–Terminal Angles and Reference Angles
- ✓ Writing Each Measure in Radians
- ✓ Writing Each Measure in Degrees
- ✓ Evaluating Each Trigonometric Expression
- ✓ Missing Sides and Angles of a Right Triangle
- ✓ Arc Length and Sector Area

Mathematics is like checkers in being suitable for the young, not too difficult, amusing, and without peril to the state. – Plato

Trig ratios of General Angles

✏️ *Use a calculator to find each. Round your answers to the nearest ten–thousandth.*

1) sin − 150°

2) sin 120°

3) cos 315°

4) cos 120°

5) sin 180°

6) sin − 300°

✏️ *Find the exact value of each trigonometric function. Some may be undefined.*

7) sec -120

8) tan $-\dfrac{3\pi}{4}$

11) cos $\dfrac{\pi}{6}$

12) cot $\dfrac{\pi}{3}$

13) sec $-\dfrac{3\pi}{2}$

14) tan $-\dfrac{2\pi}{3}$

Sketch Each Angle in Standard Position

✏️ *Draw the angle with the given measure in standard position.*

1) 140°

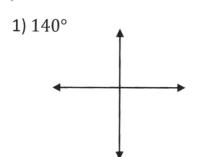

2) −250°

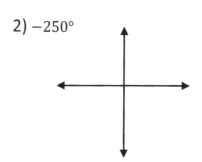

3) 610°

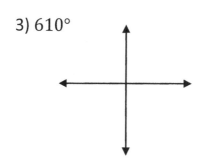

4) $\frac{55\pi}{12}$

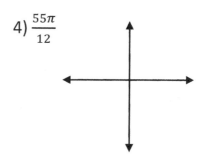

5) $\frac{5\pi}{6}$

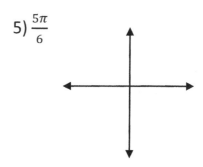

6) $-\frac{13\pi}{6}$

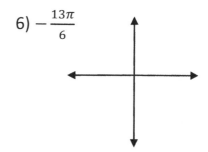

Finding Co-terminal Angles and Reference Angles

✎ *Find a conterminal angle between 0° and 360°.*

1) $-480°$

2) $680°$

3) $-335°$

4) $-430°$

✎ *Find a conterminal angle between 0 and 2π for each given angle.*

5) $\dfrac{11\pi}{3}$

6) $-\dfrac{5\pi}{6}$

7) $-\dfrac{2\pi}{45}$

8) $\dfrac{14\pi}{3}$

✎ *Find the reference angle.*

9)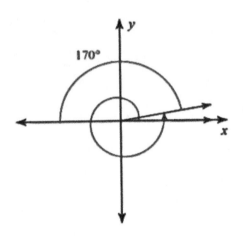

170°

10)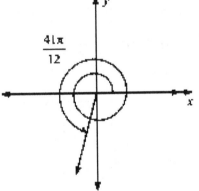

$\dfrac{41\pi}{12}$

Writing Each Measure in Radians

✍ *Convert each degree measure into radians.*

1) −120°

2) 220°

3) 160°

4) 920°

5) −200°

6) 230°

7) 265°

8) 20°

9) 420°

10) 30°

11) 297°

12) 500°

13) 504°

14) −130°

15) −260°

16) 423°

17) 440°

18) −190°

19) 250°

20) 350°

Writing Each Measure in Degrees

✎ *Convert each radian measure into degrees.*

1) $\dfrac{\pi}{60}$

2) $\dfrac{12\pi}{30}$

3) $\dfrac{13\pi}{6}$

4) $\dfrac{\pi}{3}$

5) $-\dfrac{10\pi}{9}$

6) $\dfrac{12\pi}{3}$

7) $-\dfrac{16\pi}{3}$

8) $-\dfrac{8\pi}{20}$

9) $\dfrac{5\pi}{6}$

10) $\dfrac{2\pi}{9}$

11) $\dfrac{7\pi}{6}$

12) $\dfrac{15\pi}{60}$

13) $\dfrac{11\pi}{4}$

14) $-\dfrac{22\pi}{11}$

15) $\dfrac{14\pi}{9}$

16) $-\dfrac{41\pi}{60}$

17) $-\dfrac{17\pi}{6}$

18) $\dfrac{32\pi}{18}$

19) $-\dfrac{4\pi}{3}$

20) $\dfrac{5\pi}{9}$

Evaluating Each Trigonometric Function

Find the exact value of each trigonometric function.

1) cos 315°

2) $\tan \frac{\pi}{6}$

3) $\tan \frac{\pi}{6}$

4) $\cot -\frac{5\pi}{6}$

5) $\cos \frac{2\pi}{3}$

6) cos − 240°

7) sin 480°

8) tan 480°

9) cot 390°

10) tan 405°

Use the given point on the terminal side of angle θ to find the value of the trigonometric function indicated.

11) sin θ; (− 6, 4)

12) cos θ; (2, − 2)

13) cot θ; (− 7, $\sqrt{15}$)

14) cos θ; (− 2$\sqrt{3}$, − 2)

15) sin θ; (− $\sqrt{7}$, 3)

16) tan θ; (− 11, − 2)

Missing Sides and Angles of a Right Triangle

✎ Find the value of each trigonometric ratio as fractions in their simplest form.

1) tan A

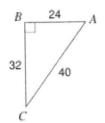

2) sin X

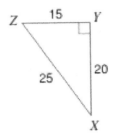

✎ Find the missing side. Round answers to the nearest tenth.

3)

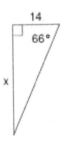

4)

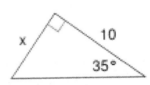

5)

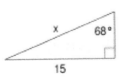

6)

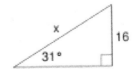

Arc Length and Sector Area

✎ Find the length of each arc. Round your answers to the nearest tenth.

1) r = 12 cm, θ = 65°

2) r = 10 ft, θ = 95°

3) r = 33 ft, θ = 90°

4) r = 16 m, θ = 86°

✎ Find area of a sector. Do not round.

5)

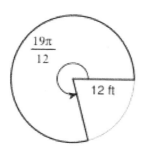

7)

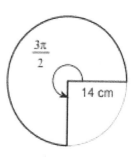

6)

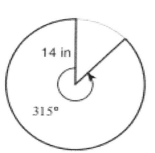

8)

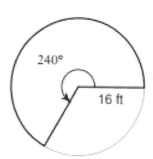

Answers of Worksheets – Chapter 11

Trig Ratios of General Angles

1) $-\dfrac{1}{2}$

2) $\dfrac{\sqrt{3}}{2}$

3) $\dfrac{\sqrt{2}}{2}$

4) $-\dfrac{1}{2}$

5) 0

6) $\dfrac{\sqrt{3}}{2}$

7) -2

8) 1

9) $\dfrac{\sqrt{3}}{2}$

10) $\dfrac{\sqrt{3}}{3}$

11) Undefined

12) $\sqrt{3}$

Sketch Each Angle in Standard Position

1) 140

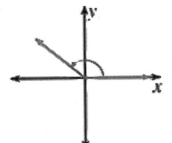

4) $\dfrac{55\pi}{12}$

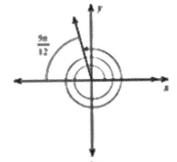

2) −250

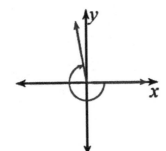

5) $\dfrac{5\pi}{6}$

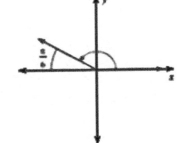

3) 610

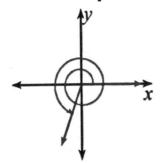

6) $\dfrac{11\pi}{6}$

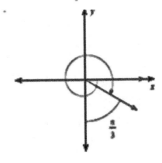

TSI Math Workbook

Finding Co–Terminal Angles and Reference Angles

1) 240°
2) 3200°
3) 25°
4) 290°
5) $\frac{5\pi}{3}$
6) $\frac{7\pi}{6}$
7) $\frac{88\pi}{45}$
8) $\frac{2\pi}{3}$
9) 370°
10) $\frac{5\pi}{12}$

Writing Each Measure in Radians

1) $-\frac{2\pi}{3}$
2) $\frac{11\pi}{9}$
3) $\frac{8\pi}{9}$
4) $\frac{46\pi}{9}$
5) $-\frac{10\pi}{9}$
6) $\frac{23\pi}{18}$
7) $\frac{53\pi}{36}$
8) $\frac{\pi}{9}$
9) $\frac{7\pi}{3}$
10) $\frac{\pi}{6}$
11) $\frac{33\pi}{2}$
12) $\frac{25\pi}{9}$
13) $\frac{14\pi}{5}$
14) $-\frac{13\pi}{18}$
15) $-\frac{13\pi}{9}$
16) $\frac{47\pi}{2}$
17) $\frac{22\pi}{9}$
18) $-\frac{19\pi}{18}$
19) $\frac{25\pi}{18}$
20) $\frac{35\pi}{18}$

Writing Each Measure in Degrees

1) 3°
2) 72°
3) 390°
4) 60°
5) −200°
6) 720°
7) −960°
8) −72°
9) 150°
10) 40°
11) 210°
12) 45°
13) 495°
14) −360°
15) 280°
16) −123°
17) −510°
18) 320°
19) −240°
20) 100°

Evaluating Each Trigonometric Expression

1) $\frac{\sqrt{2}}{2}$
2) $-\frac{\sqrt{3}}{3}$
3) $\frac{\sqrt{3}}{3}$
4) $-\sqrt{3}$
5) $-\frac{1}{2}$
6) $-\frac{1}{2}$

7) $\frac{\sqrt{3}}{2}$

8) $-\sqrt{3}$

9) $\sqrt{3}$

10) 1

11) $\frac{2\sqrt{13}}{13}$

12) $-\sqrt{2}$

13) $-\frac{7\sqrt{15}}{15}$

14) $-\frac{\sqrt{3}}{2}$

15) $\frac{3}{4}$

16) $\frac{2}{11}$

Missing Sides and Angles of a Right Triangle

1) $\frac{4}{3}$

2) $\frac{3}{5}$

3) 31.4

4) 7.0

5) 16.2

6) 31.1

Arc Length and Sector Area

1) 74 cm

2) 17 ft

3) 52 ft

4) 24 m

5) 114π ft^2

6) $\frac{343\pi}{2}$ in^2

7) 147π cm^2

8) $\frac{512\pi}{3}$ ft^2

Chapter 12: Geometry - Plane and solid Figures

Topics that you'll learn in this chapter:

✓ The Pythagorean Theorem

✓ Area of Triangles and Trapezoids

✓ Area and Circumference of Circles

✓ Area and Perimeter of Polygons

✓ Area of Squares, Rectangles, and Parallelograms

✓ Volume of Cubes, Rectangle Prisms, and Cylinder

✓ Surface Area of Cubes, Rectangle Prisms, and Cylinder

Mathematics is, as it were, a sensuous logic, and relates to philosophy as do the arts, music, and plastic art to poetry. – K. Shekel

Transformations: Translations, Rotations, and Reflections

🖉 Graph the image of the figure using the transformation given.

1) translation: 4 units right and 1 unit down

2) translation: 4 units right and 2 unit up

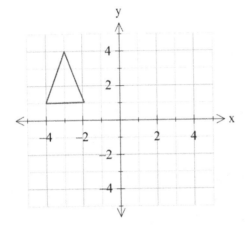
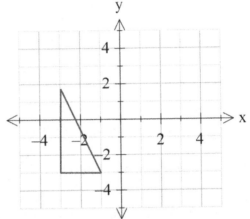

3) rotation 90° counterclockwise about the origin

4) rotation 180° about the origin

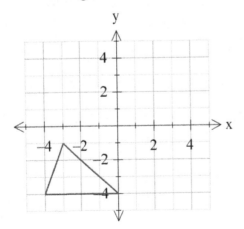
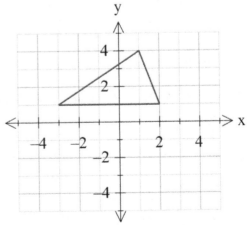

The Pythagorean Theorem

✎ Do the following lengths form a right triangle?

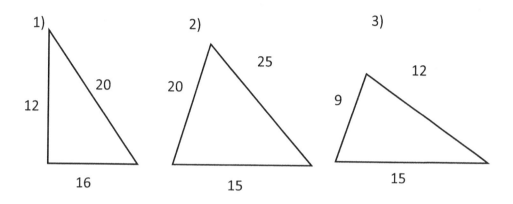

✎ Find each missing length to the nearest tenth.

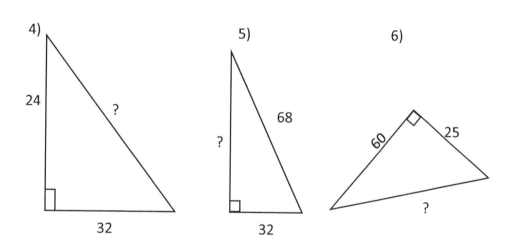

Area of Triangles

✏️ **Find the area of each.**

1)

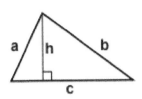

c = 12 mi

h = 4.5 mi

2)

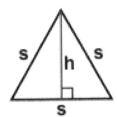

s = 8 m

h = 9.4 m

3)

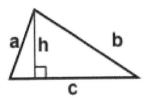

a = 4 m

b = 11 m

c = 16 m

h = 13.6 m

4)

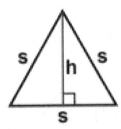

s = 6 m

h = 6.71 m

Area of Trapezoids

Calculate the area for each trapezoid.

1)

2)

3)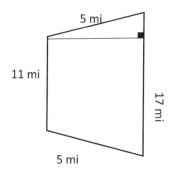

4)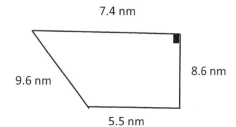

Area and Perimeter of Quadrilateral.

🔍 Find the area and perimeter of each

1)
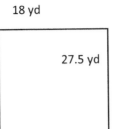

2)
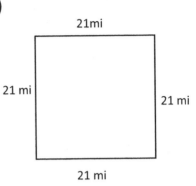

3)
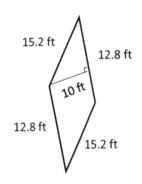

4)
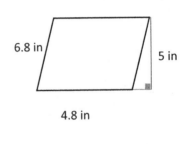

5)
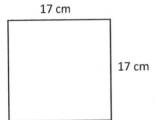

6)
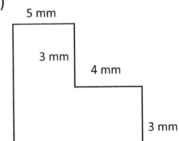

Find the perimeter of each shape.

7)

8)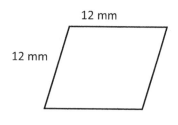

9)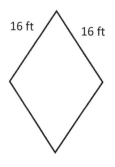

10)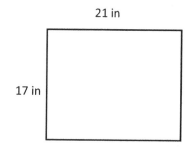

11)

12)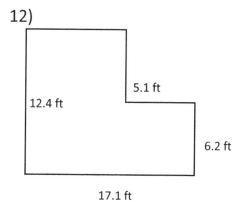

Area and Circumference of Circles

✏️ Find the area and circumference of each. ($\pi = 3.14$)

1) 2.5 cm (radius)

2) 4 in (radius)

3) 9 km (radius)

4) 5.5 m (radius)

5) 12 m (diameter)

6) 6 cm (diameter)

7) 7 cm (diameter)

8) 3 in (diameter)

Volume of Cubes

✎ Find the volume of each.

1)
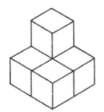

2)
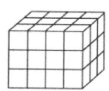

3)
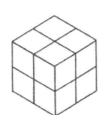

4)

5)
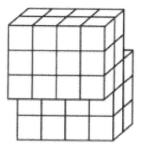

6)
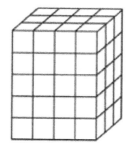

Volume of Rectangle Prisms

✏️ **Find the volume of each of the rectangular prisms.**

1)
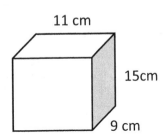

2)
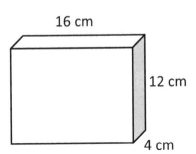

3)
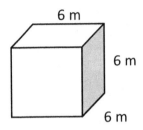

4)
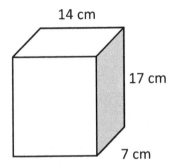

5)
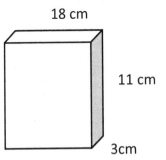

6)
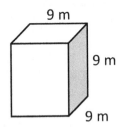

Surface Area of Cubes

✏️ Find the surface of each cube.

1)

2)

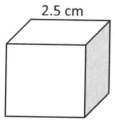

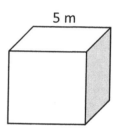

3)

4)

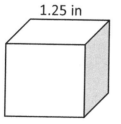

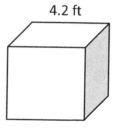

5)

6)

Surface Area of a Rectangle Prism

✏️ Find the surface of each prism.

1)

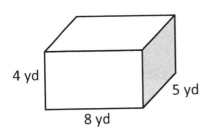

2)

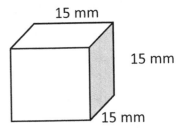

3)

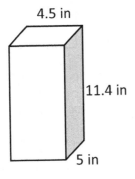

4)

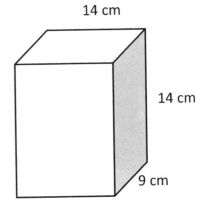

Volume of a Cylinder

🖎 Find the volume of each cylinder. ($\pi = 3.14$)

1)
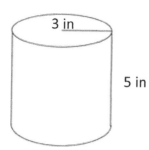

2)
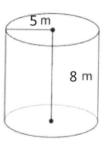

3)
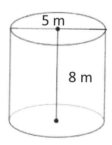

4)
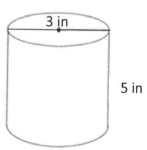

5)
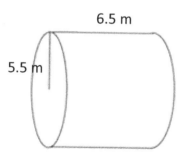

6)
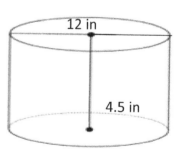

Surface Area of a Cylinder

✏️ Find the surface of each cylinder. ($\pi = 3.14$)

1)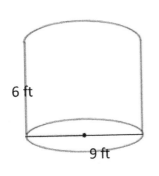
6 ft
9 ft

2)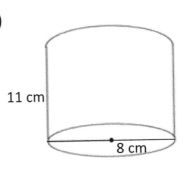
11 cm
8 cm

3)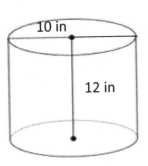
10 in
12 in

4)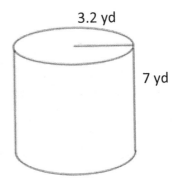
3.2 yd
7 yd

5)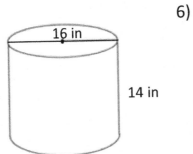
16 in
14 in

6)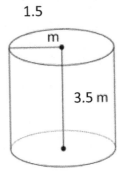
1.5 m
3.5 m

TSI Math Workbook

Volume of Pyramids and Cones

✏️ **Find the volume of each figure** ($\pi = 3.14$).

1)

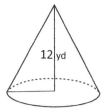

2)

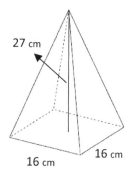

3)

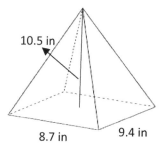

4)

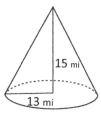

5)

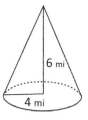

6)

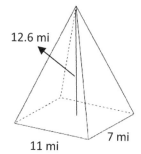

Surface Area of Pyramids and Cones

✎ Find the surface area of each figure ($\pi = 3.14$).

1)
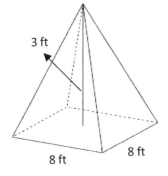

2)
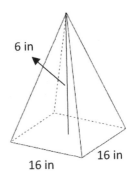

3)
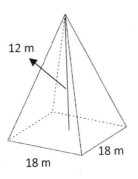

4)
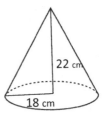

5)
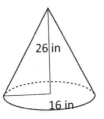

6)
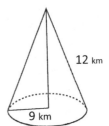

Answers of Worksheets – Chapter 12

Transformations: Translations, Rotations, and Reflections

1)
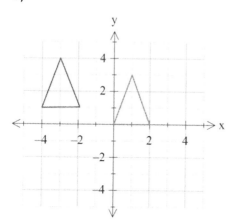

2)
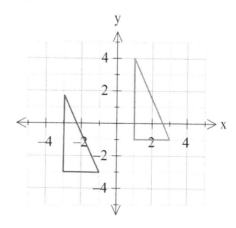

3) rotation 90° counterclockwise about the origin

4) rotation 180° about the origin

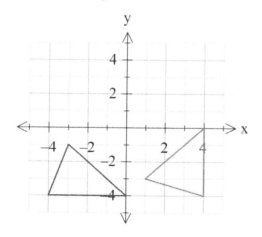

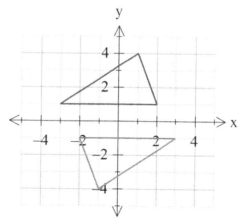

The Pythagorean Theorem

1) yes   3) yes   5) 60
2) yes   4) 40   6) 65

Area of Triangles

1) 27 mi^2 3) 108.8 m^2
2) 37.6 m^2 4) 20.13 m^2

TSI Math Workbook

Area of Trapezoids

1) 84 cm^2
2) 252 m^2
3) 56 mi^2
4) 55.47 nm^2

Area of Squares, Rectangles, and Parallelograms

1) Area: 495 m^2, P: 91
2) Area: 441 mm^2, Perimeter: 84
3) Area: 128 ft^2, Perimeter: 56 ft
4) Area: 24 in^2, Perimeter: 23.2in
5) Area: 289 cm^2, Perimeter 68 cm
6) Area: 42mm^2, Perimeter:30 mi
7) P: 42 m
8) P: 48 mm
9) P: 64 ft
10) P: 76 in
11) P: 56 cm
12) P: 59 ft

Area and Circumference of Circles

1) Area: 19.63 cm^2, Circumference: 15.7 cm.
2) Area: 50.24 in^2, Circumference: 25.12 in.
3) Area: 254.34 km^2, Circumference: 56.52 km.
4) Area: 94.99 m^2, Circumference: 34.54 m.
5) Area: 113.04 m^2, Circumference: 37.68 m
6) Area: 28.26 cm^2, Circumference: 18.84 cm.
7) Area: 38.47 cm^2, Circumference: 21.98 cm.
8) Area: 7.07 in^2, Circumference: 9.42 in.

Perimeter of Polygons

1) 710.6 yd^2
2) 729 mi^2
3) 105.7 ft^2
4) 23.6 in^2

Volumes of Cubes

1) 5   3) 8   5) 44

2) 36   4) 4   6) 60

Volume of Rectangle Prisms

1) 1485 cm³   3) 216 m³   5) 594 cm³

2) 768 cm³   4) 1666 cm³   6) 729 cm³

Surface Area of a Cube

1) 54 mm²   3) 37.5 cm²   5) 9.375 in²

2) 726 mm²   4) 150 m²   6) 105.84 ft²

Surface Area of a Prism

1) 184 yd²   3) 261.6 in²

2) 1350 mm²   4) 896 cm²

Volume of a Cylinder

1) 141.3 cm³   3) 157 m³   5) 617.4 m³

2) 628 cm³   4) 35.325 m³   6) 508.68 m³

Surface Area of a Cylinder

1) 296.73 ft²   3) 533.8 in²   5) 1105.28 in²

2) 376.8 cm²   4) 204.98 yd²   6) 47.1 m²

Volume of Pyramids and Cones

1) 615.4 yd³   4) 2,653.3 mi³

2) 1,024 cm³   5) 100.5 in³

3) 286.2 mi³   6) 323.4 mi³

Surface Area of Pyramids and Cones

1) 144 in³   4) 2,623.96 m3

2) 576 in2   5) 2,337.601 ft2

3) 864 m3   6) 678.24 km

Chapter 13:

Statistics and Probability

Topics that you'll learn in this chapter:

- ✓ Mean, Median, Mode, and Range of the Given Data
- ✓ Box and Whisker Plots
- ✓ Histogerams
- ✓ Bar Graph
- ✓ Stem– And– Leaf Plot
- ✓ The Pie Graph or Circle Graph
- ✓ Dot and Scatter Plots
- ✓ Probability of Simple Events
- ✓ Experimental Probability
- ✓ Independent and Dependent Events Word Problems
- ✓ Factorials
- ✓ Permutations and Combination

Mathematics is no more computation than typing is literature.

— John Allen Paulos

Mean and Median

✎ *Find Mean and Median of the Given Data.*

1) 8, 12, 5, 3, 2

2) 3, 6, 3, 7, 4, 13

3) 13, 5, 1, 7, 9

4) 6, 4, 2, 7, 3, 2

5) 6, 5, 7, 5, 7, 1, 11

6) 6, 1, 4, 4, 9, 2, 19

7) 12, 4, 1, 5, 9, 7, 7, 19

8) 18, 9, 5, 4, 9, 6, 12

9) 28, 25, 15, 16, 32, 44, 71

10) 10, 5, 1, 5, 4, 5, 8, 10

11) 18, 15, 30, 64, 42, 11

12) 44, 33, 56, 78, 41, 84

✎ *Solve.*

13) In a javelin throw competition, five athletics score 56, 58, 63, 57 and 61 meters. What are their Mean and Median? _____

14) Eva went to shop and bought 3 apples, 5 peaches, 8 bananas, 1 pineapple and 3 melons. What are the Mean and Median of her purchase? _____

TSI Math Workbook

Mode and Range

✎ *Find Mode and Rage of the Given Data.*

1) 8, 2, 5, 9, 1, 2
Mode: _____ Range: _____

2) 6, 6, 2, 3, 6, 3, 9, 12
Mode: _____ Range: _____

3) 4, 4, 3, 9, 7, 9, 4, 6, 4
Mode: _____ Range: _____

4) 12, 9, 2, 9, 3, 2, 9, 5
Mode: _____ Range: _____

5) 9, 5, 9, 5, 8, 9, 8
Mode: _____ Range: _____

6) 0, 1, 4, 10, 9, 2, 9, 1, 5, 1
Mode: _____ Range: _____

7) 6, 5, 6, 9, 7, 7, 5, 4, 3, 5
Mode: _____ Range: _____

8) 7, 5, 4, 9, 6, 7, 7, 5, 2
Mode: _____ Range: _____

9) 2, 2, 5, 6, 2, 4, 7, 6, 4, 9
Mode: _____ Range: _____

10) 7, 5, 2, 5, 4, 5, 8, 10
Mode: _____ Range: _____

11) 4, 1, 5, 2, 2, 12, 18, 2
Mode: _____ Range: _____

12) 6, 3, 5, 9, 6, 6, 3, 12
Mode: _____ Range: _____

✎ *Solve.*

13) A stationery sold 12 pencils, 36 red pens, 44 blue pens, 12 notebooks, 18 erasers, 34 rulers and 32 color pencils. What are the Mode and Range for the stationery sells?
Mode: _____   Range: _____

14) In an English test, eight students score 14, 13, 17, 11, 19, 20, 14 and 15. What are their Mode and Range?

_____

Histograms

Use the following Graph to complete the table.

Day	Distance (km)
1	
2	

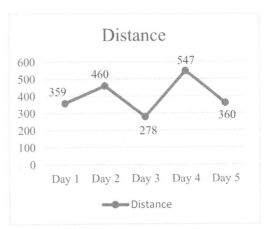

The following table shows the number of births in the US from 2007 to 2012 (in millions).

Year	Number of births (in millions)
2007	4.32
2008	4.25
2009	4.13
2010	4
2011	3.95
2012	3.95

Draw a histogram for the table.

Box and Whisker Plot

✎ Make box and whisker plots for the given data.

1, 5, 18, 8, 3, 11, 13, 12, 24, 17, 10, 15, 25

Bar Graph

✎ Graph the given information as a bar graph.

Day	Sale House
Monday	5
Tuesday	7
Wednesday	9
Thursday	8
Friday	0
Saturday	3
Sunday	4

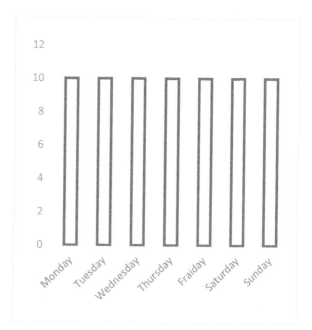

Dot plots

A survey of "How many pets each person owned?" has these results:

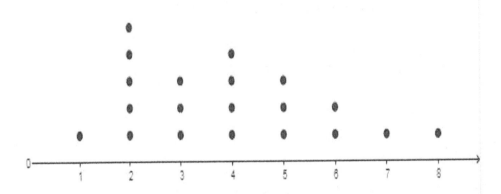

1) How many people have at least 4 pets?

2) How many people have 5 and 6 pets?

3) What is the most common number of pets?

4) How many people have 3 or less than 3 pets?

5) How many people have more than 6 pets?

Scatter Plots

Construct a scatter plot.

x	1	2	3	4	4.5	5
y	5	3.5	4	2	7	1.5

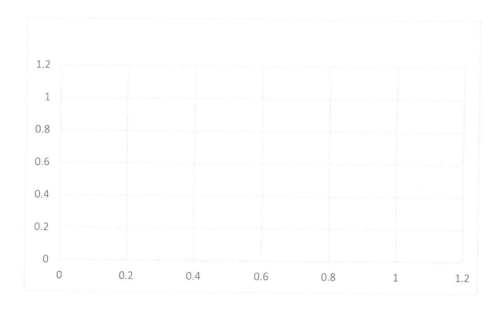

Stem–And–Leaf Plot

✎ Make stem ad leaf plots for the given data.

1) 22, 24, 27, 21, 52, 24, 58, 57, 29, 24, 19, 12

2) 11, 45, 34, 18, 15, 11, 32, 41, 40, 30, 45, 35

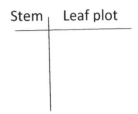

3) 112, 87, 96, 85, 100, 117, 92, 114, 88, 112, 98, 107

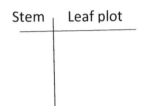

4) 63, 50, 104, 63, 72, 56, 109 63, 75, 59, 63, 108, 79

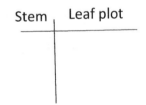

The Pie Graph or Circle Graph

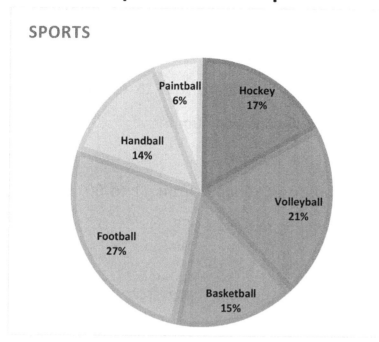

Favorite Sports:

1) What percentage of pie graph is Handball?

2) What percentage of pie graph is Hockey?

3) Which sport is the most?

4) Which sport is the least?

5) What percentage of pie graph is Volleyball?

6) What percentage of pie not football and volleyball?

Probability of Simple Events

✏️ Solve.

1) A number is chosen at random from 25 to 34. Find the probability of selecting an even number.

2) A number is chosen at random from 21 to 60. Find the probability of selecting multiples of 5.

3) Find the probability of selecting 4 aces from a deck of card.

4) A number is chosen at random from 10 to 19. Find the probability of selecting of 11 and factors of 3.

5) What probability of selecting a ball less than 11 from 40 different bingo balls?

6) Find the probability of not selecting a king from a deck of card.

Experimental Probability

One cube	Frequency
1	6
2	9
3	5
4	7
5	8
6	5

1) Theoretically if you roll a number cube 24 times, how many times would you expect to roll the number two?

2) How many times did you roll the number two in the experiment?

3) Is there any difference between theoretical and experimental probability?

4) What is the theoretical probability for rolling a number greater than 4?

5) What was the experimental probability of rolling a number greater than 3?

Factorials

Determine the value for each expression.

1) $5!$

2) $\dfrac{7!}{10!}$

3) $\dfrac{10!}{6!}$

4) $\dfrac{n!}{(n-3)!}$

5) $\dfrac{12!}{8!4!}$

6) $\dfrac{45!}{44!}$

7) $\dfrac{100!}{101!}$

8) $\dfrac{(M+1)!}{(M-1)!}$

9) $\dfrac{15!}{10!}$

10) $\dfrac{28!}{25!}$

11) $\dfrac{0!4!}{1!0!}$

12) $\dfrac{22!}{20!}$

13) $\dfrac{(5.2)!}{(4.2)!}$

14) $7! + 3!$

Permutations

Evaluate each expression.

1) $5\ _4P_1$

2) $_7P_3$

3) $_8P_5$

4) $12 +\ _{10}P_3$

5) $P(5,3)$

6) $P(6,2)$

7) $(_5P_4)$

8) $\frac{1}{2}(_{12}P_1)$

9) $_4P_0$

10) $_0P_0$

11) $_4P_4$

12) $_9P_3$

13) How many possible 7–digit telephone numbers are there? Someone left their umbrella on the subway and we need to track them down.

14) With repetition allowed, how many ways can one choose 6 out of 15 things?

Combination

✎ List all possible combinations.

1) 1, 4, 3, 5, taken four at a time

2) A, B, D, taken two at a time

✎ Evaluate each expression.

3) $_4C_1$

4) $_7C_3$

5) $\binom{12}{5}$

6) $3 + \binom{21}{14}$

7) $C(5,3)$

8) $C(6,2)$

9) $5(_{13}C_9)$

10) $\frac{1}{2}(_{12}C_1)$

11) $_5C_0$

12) $_0C_0$

13) $_6C_6$

14) $_{18}C_{17}$

Answers of Worksheets – Chapter 13

Mean and Median

1) Mean: 6, Median: 5
2) Mean: 6, Median: 5
3) Mean: 7, Median: 7
4) Mean: 4, Median: 3.5
5) Mean: 6, Median: 6
6) Mean: 8, Median: 4
7) Mean: 8, Median: 7
8) Mean: 9, Median: 9
9) Mean: 33, Median: 28
10) Mean: 6, Median: 5
11) Mean: 30, Median: 24
12) Mean: 56, Median: 50
13) Mean: 59, Median: 58
14) Mean: 4, Median: 3

Mode and Range

1) Mode: 2, Range: 8
2) Mode: 6, Range: 10
3) Mode: 4, Range: 6
4) Mode: 9, Range: 10
5) Mode: 9, Range: 4
6) Mode: 1, Range: 10
7) Mode: 5, Range: 6
8) Mode: 7, Range: 7
9) Mode: 2, Range: 7
10) Mode: 5, Range: 8
11) Mode: 2, Range: 17
12) Mode: 6, Range: 9
13) Mode: 12, Range: 32
14) Mode: 14, Range: 9

Histograms

Day	Distance (km)
1	359
2	460
3	278
4	547
5	360

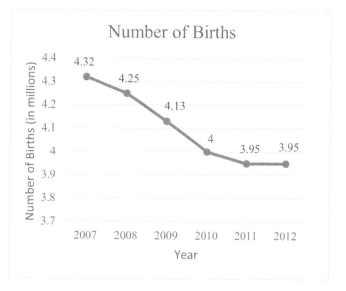

Box and Whisker Plots

1, 3, 5, 8, 10, 11, 12, 13, 15, 17, 18, 24, 25

Maximum: 25, Minimum: 1, Q_1: 6.5, Q_2: 12, Q_3: 17.5

Dot plots

1) 11
2) 5
3) 2
4) 9
5) 2

Bar Graph

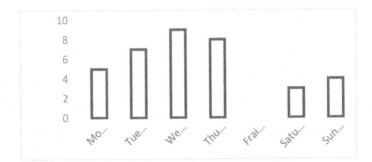

Scatter Plots

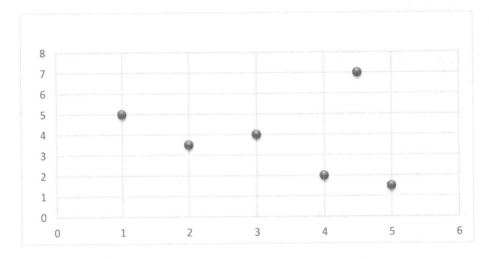

TSI Math Workbook

Stem–And–Leaf Plot

1)
Stem	leaf
1	2 9
2	1 2 4 4 4 7 9
5	2 7 8

2)
Stem	leaf
1	1 1 5 8
3	0 2 4 5
4	0 1 5 5

3)
Stem	leaf
8	5 7 8
9	2 6 8
10	0 7
11	2 2 4 7

4)
Stem	leaf
5	0 6 9
6	3 3 3 3
7	2 5 9
10	4 8 9

The Pie Graph or Circle Graph

1) 14%
2) Football
3) Paintball
4) 17%
5) 21%
6) 52%

Probability of simple events

1) $\frac{1}{2}$
2) $\frac{1}{5}$
3) $\frac{1}{13}$
4) $\frac{2}{5}$
5) $\frac{1}{4}$
6) $\frac{12}{13}$

Experimental Probability

1) 4
2) 9
3) yes
4) 1/3
5) 1/2

Factorials

1) 120
2) 336
3) 5,040
4) $n(n-1)(n-2)$
5) 495
6) 45
7) $\frac{1}{100}$
8) $M(M-1)$
9) 360,360
10) 19,656
11) 24
12) 462
13) 5.2
14) 5046

Permutations
1) 20
2) 210
3) 6720
4) 732
5) 60
6) 30
7) 120
8) 6
9) 1
10) 1
11) 24
12) 504
13) 10^7
14) 15^6

Combination
1) 1435
2) AB, AD, BD
3) 4
4) 35
5) 792
6) 116,283
7) 10
8) 15
9) 715
10) 495
11) 6
12) 1
13) 1
14) 18

TSI Math Test Review

The Texas Success Initiative Assessment, is known as the TSI, is a test to determine the appropriate level of college course work for an incoming student. In essence, it is a broad and quick assessment of students' academic abilities.

The TSI test consists of three separate exams:

- ✓ Mathematics
- ✓ Reading
- ✓ Writing

The mathematics portion of the TSI test contains 20 questions. The test covers data analysis, geometry, and algebra on both intermediate and basic levels.

Students are not allowed to use calculator when taking a TSI assessment. A pop-up calculator is embedded in the test for some questions.

In this section, there are two complete TSI Mathematics Tests. Take these tests to see what score you'll be able to receive on a real TSI test.

The hardest arithmetic to master is that which enables us to count our blessings. ~Eric Hoffer

Time to Test

Time to refine your skill with a practice examination

Take a practice TSI Math Test to simulate the test day experience. After you've finished, score your test using the answer key.

Before You Start

- You'll need a pencil, a calculator and a timer to take the test.
- After you've finished the test, review the answer key to see where you went wrong.

Good Luck!

TSI Math Practice Test Answer Sheets

Remove (or photocopy) these answer sheets and use them to complete the practice tests.

TSI Practice Test

1 Ⓐ Ⓑ Ⓒ Ⓓ		1 Ⓐ Ⓑ Ⓒ Ⓓ	
2 Ⓐ Ⓑ Ⓒ Ⓓ		2 Ⓐ Ⓑ Ⓒ Ⓓ	
3 Ⓐ Ⓑ Ⓒ Ⓓ		3 Ⓐ Ⓑ Ⓒ Ⓓ	
4 Ⓐ Ⓑ Ⓒ Ⓓ		4 Ⓐ Ⓑ Ⓒ Ⓓ	
5 Ⓐ Ⓑ Ⓒ Ⓓ		5 Ⓐ Ⓑ Ⓒ Ⓓ	
6 Ⓐ Ⓑ Ⓒ Ⓓ		6 Ⓐ Ⓑ Ⓒ Ⓓ	
7 Ⓐ Ⓑ Ⓒ Ⓓ		7 Ⓐ Ⓑ Ⓒ Ⓓ	
8 Ⓐ Ⓑ Ⓒ Ⓓ		8 Ⓐ Ⓑ Ⓒ Ⓓ	
9 Ⓐ Ⓑ Ⓒ Ⓓ		9 Ⓐ Ⓑ Ⓒ Ⓓ	
10 Ⓐ Ⓑ Ⓒ Ⓓ		10 Ⓐ Ⓑ Ⓒ Ⓓ	

www.MathNotion.com

TSI Math Practice Test 1

Mathematics

2 Sections

- ❖ 20 Questions.
- ❖ Total time for this test: No Limit Time.
- ❖ You may NOT use a calculator on this Section.

Administered Month Year

Section 1:

Arithmetic and Elementary Algebra

1) If two angles in a triangle measure 75 degrees and 43degrees, what is the value of the third angle?

   A. 34 degrees

   B. 44 degrees

   C. 62 degrees

   D. 118 degrees

2) If $2.05 < x \leq 4.04$, then x cannot be equal to:

   A. 3.004

   B. 2.06

   C. 3.07

   D. 4.40

3) What is the area of an isosceles right triangle that has one leg that measures 6 cm?

   A. 16cm

   B18 cm

   C. $8\sqrt{2}$ cm

   D. 72 cm

4) $\frac{1}{6b^2} + \frac{1}{6b} = \frac{1}{b^2}$, then $b = ?$

   A. $-\frac{16}{15}$

   B. 5

   C. $-\frac{15}{16}$

   D. 8

5) Which of the following expressions is equivalent to $12 - \frac{2}{3}x \geq 14$

   A. $x \geq -3$

   B. $x \leq -3$

   C. $x \geq 24\frac{1}{3}$

   D. $x \leq 24\frac{1}{3}$

6) $(x + 8)(x + 5) =$

   A. $x^2 + 13x + 12$

   B. $2x + 13x + 12$

   C. $x^2 + 40x + 13$

   D. $x^2 + 13x + 40$

7) Which of the following is a factor of both $x^2 + x - 12$ and $x^2 - 7x + 12$?

   A. $(x - 4)$

   B. $(x + 4)$

   C. $(x - 3)$

   D. $(x + 3)$

8) If x is a positive integer divisible by 6, and $x < 60$, what is the greatest possible value of x?

   A. 42

   B. 48

   C. 24

   D. 58

9) $x^2 - 81 = 0$, x could equal to:

   A. 6

   B. 8

   C. 9

   D. 32

10) If $a = 6$, what is the value of b in this equation?

$$b = \frac{a^2}{4} + 4$$

   A. 22

   B. 13

   C. 20

   D. 25

Section 2:

College–Level Mathematics

1) $\dfrac{\sqrt{27a^5b^3}}{\sqrt{3ab^2}} = ?$

   A. $3a^2\sqrt{b}$

   B. $2b^2\sqrt{a}$

   C. $3b^2\sqrt{a}$

   D. $-3a^2\sqrt{b}$

2) $\tan\left(-\dfrac{\pi}{4}\right) = ?$

   A. 1

   B. $-\dfrac{\sqrt{2}}{2}$

   C. $\dfrac{\sqrt{2}}{2}$

   D. -1

3) Which of the following point is the solution of the system of equations?

$$\begin{cases} 4x + y = 8 \\ 8x - 6y = -16 \end{cases}$$

   A. (1, 2)

   B. (2, 2)

   C. (1, 4)

   D. (0, 2)

4) Ella (E) is 5 years older than her friend Ava (A) who is 4 years younger than her sister Sofia (S). If E, A and S denote their ages, which one of the following represents the given information?

A. $\begin{cases} E = A + 5 \\ S = A - 4 \end{cases}$

B. $\begin{cases} E = A + 5 \\ A = S + 4 \end{cases}$

C. $\begin{cases} A = E + 5 \\ S = A - 4 \end{cases}$

D. $\begin{cases} E = A + 5 \\ A = S - 4 \end{cases}$

5) Find the Center and Radius of the graph $(x - 4)^2 + (y + 5)^2 = 18$

A. $(4, 5), \sqrt{2}$

B. $(4, -5), 3\sqrt{2}$

C. $(-4, 5), 3\sqrt{2}$

D. $(4, -5), \sqrt{2}$

6) The cost, in thousands of dollars, of producing x thousands of textbooks is $C(x) = x^2 + 5x + 30$. The revenue, also in thousands of dollars, is $R(x) = 6x$. Find the profit or loss if 3,000 textbooks are produced. (profit = revenue − cost)

A. $24,000 loss

B. $36,000 profit

C. $3,000 profit

D. $36,000 loss

7) $\frac{|3+x|}{7} \leq 6$, then $x = ?$

   A. $-45 \leq x \leq 35$

   B. $-45 \leq x \leq 39$

   C. $-32 \leq x \leq 38$

   D. $-42 \leq x \leq 42$

8) Find the slope–intercept form of the graph $4x - 5y = -12$

   A. $y = -\frac{5}{4}x - \frac{12}{5}$

   B. $y = -\frac{4}{5}x + 12$

   C. $y = \frac{4}{5}x + \frac{12}{5}$

   D. $y = \frac{5}{4}x - 12$

9) If $f(x) = 4 + x$ and $g(x) = -x^2 - 1 - 3x$, then find $(g - f)(x)$?

   A. $x^2 - 4x - 5$

   B. $x^2 - 4x + 5$

   C. $-x^2 - 4x + 5$

   D. $-x^2 - 4x - 5$

10) Suppose a triangle has the dimensions indicated below:

   Then Sin B = ?

   A. $\frac{3}{5}$ C. $\frac{4}{3}$

   B. $\frac{5}{6}$ D. $\frac{3}{4}$

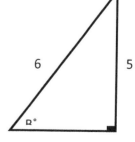

TSI Math Practice Test 2

Mathematics

2 Sections

- ❖ 20 Questions.
- ❖ Total time for this test: No Limit Time.
- ❖ You may NOT use a calculator on this Section.

Administered Month Year

Section 1:

Arithmetic and Elementary Algebra

1) $7^5 \times 7^8 = ?$

   A. 7^{23}

   B. $7^{0.82}$

   C. 7^{13}

   D. 1^7

2) If $11 + 2x \leq 15$, then $x \leq ?$

   A. $2x$

   B. 2

   C. -2

   D. $12x$

3) Last Friday Jacob had $32.52. Over the weekend he received some money for cleaning the attic. He now has $44. How much money did he receive?

   A. $76.52

   B. $11.48

   C. $32.08

   D. $12.58

4) Simplify $\dfrac{\dfrac{1}{2}-\dfrac{x+5}{4}}{\dfrac{x^2}{2}-\dfrac{5}{2}}$

A. $\dfrac{3-x}{x^2-10}$

B. $\dfrac{3-x}{2x^2-10}$

C. $\dfrac{3+x}{x^2-10}$

D. $\dfrac{-3-x}{2x^2-10}$

5) 15 is what percent of 75?

   A. 20%

   B. 30%

   C. 40%

   D. 50%

6) What is 2364.47245 rounded to the nearest tenth?

   A. 2364.472

   B. 2364.5

   C. 2364

   D2364.47

7) $\sqrt{58}$ is between which two whole numbers?

   A. 4and 5

   B. 5 and 6

   C. 7nd 8

   D. 6 and 7

8) Liam's average (arithmetic mean) on two mathematics tests is 8. What should Liam's score be on the next test to have an overall of 9 for all the tests?

   A. 8

   B. 9

   C. 10

   D. 11

9) How many 3 × 3 squares can fit inside a rectangle with a height of 63 and width of 18?

   A. 48

   B. 42

   C. 62

   D. 32

10) $(x - 4)(x^2 + 6x + 2) = ?$

   A. $x^3 + 2x^2 - 22x + 16$

   B. $x^3 + 2x^2 - 22x + 8$

   C. $x^3 + 2x^2 - 22x - 8$

   D. $x^3 + 2x^2 + 16x - 15$

Section 2:

College–Level Mathematics

1) What's the reciprocal of $\frac{x^3}{12}$?

   A. $\frac{12}{x^3} - 1$

   B. $\frac{48}{x^3}$

   C. $\frac{12}{x^3} + 1$

   D. $\frac{12}{x^3}$

2) What is cos 60°?

   A. $\frac{1}{2}$

   B. $\frac{\sqrt{2}}{2}$

   C. $\frac{\sqrt{3}}{2}$

   D. $\sqrt{3}$

3) If θ is an acute angle and sin θ = $\frac{4}{5}$, then cos θ = ?

   A. −1

   B. 0

   C. $\frac{3}{5}$

   D. $\frac{5}{3}$

4) What is the solution of the following system of equations?

$$\begin{cases} -4x - y = -4 \\ 8x - 2y = 8 \end{cases}$$

A. (−1, 2)

B. (1, 0)

C. (1, 4)

D. (4, −2)

5) If $\log_2 x = 3$, then $x = ?$

A. 2^8

B. $\dfrac{3}{2}$

C. 2^4

D. 8

6) Solve the equation: $\log_4(x + 3) - \log_4(x - 3) = 1$

A. 10

B. $\dfrac{3}{10}$

C. $\dfrac{10}{3}$

D. 5

7) Solve, $|9 - (12 \div | 2 - 8 |)| = ?$

A. 5

B. −7

C. 7

D. −5

8) If $f(x) = x - \frac{7}{3}$ and f^{-1} is the inverse of $f(x)$, what is the value of $f^{-1}(2)$?

A. $\frac{10}{3}$

B. $\frac{3}{20}$

C. $\frac{13}{3}$

D. $\frac{3}{10}$

9) Find the inverse function for ln $(2x - 1)$

A. $\frac{1}{2}(e^x - 1)$

B. $(e^x + 1)$

C. $\frac{1}{2}(e^x + 1)$

D. $(e^x - 1)$

10) Solve $e^{4x + 1} = 10$

A. $\frac{\ln(10) + 1}{4}$

B. $\frac{\ln(10) - 1}{4}$

C. 4ln $(10) + 2$

D. 4ln $(10) - 2$

Answers and Explanations

TSI Math Practice Tests

Answer Key

❋ Now, it's time to review your results to see where you went wrong and what areas you need to improve!

TSI Math Practice Test

Practice Test 1		Practice Test 2	
Section 1	Section 2	Section 1	Section 2
1 C	1 A	1 C	1 D
2 D	2 D	2 B	2 A
3 B	3 C	3 B	3 C
4 B	4 D	4 D	4 B
5 B	5 B	5 A	5 D
6 D	6 D	6 B	6 D
7 C	7 B	7 C	7 C
8 B	8 C	8 D	8 C
9 C	9 D	9 A	9 C
10 B	10 B	10 C	10 B

www.MathNotion.com

TSI Math Workbook

Answers and Explanations

TSI Mathematics

Practice Tests 1

Section 1: Arithmetic and Elementary Algebra

1) Answer: C.

75° + 43° = 118°

180° − 118° = 62°

The value of the third angle is 62°.

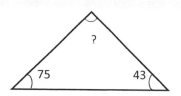

2) Answer: D.

If $2.05 < x \leq 4.04$, then x cannot be equal to 4.40. Because: $4.04 < 4.40$

3) Answer: B.

$a = 8 \Rightarrow$ area of triangle is:

$\frac{1}{2}(6 \times 6) = \frac{36}{2} = 18$ cm

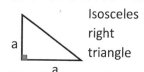

Isosceles right triangle

4) Answer: B.

$\frac{1+b}{6b^2} = \frac{1}{b^2} \Rightarrow (b \neq 0)\ b^2 + b^3 = 6b^2 \Rightarrow b^3 - 5b^2 = 0 \Rightarrow b^2(b-5) = 0 \Rightarrow b - 5 = 0 \Rightarrow b = 5$

5) Answer: B.

Simplify: $12 - \frac{2}{3}x \geq 14 \Rightarrow -\frac{2}{3}x \geq 2 \Rightarrow -x \geq 3 \Rightarrow x \leq -3$

6) Answer: D.

Use FOIL (First, Out, In, Last)

$(x + 8)(x + 5) = x^2 + 5x + 8x + 40 = x^2 + 13x + 40$

www.MathNotion.com

7) Answer: C.

Factor each trinomial $x^2 + x - 12$ and $x^2 - 7x + 12$

$x^2 + x - 12 \Rightarrow (x - 3)(x + 4)$

$x^2 - 7x + 12 \Rightarrow (x - 4)(x - 3)$

$(x - 3)$ is a factor of both trinomial.

8) Answer: B.

$\frac{42}{6} = \frac{21}{3} = 7, \quad \frac{48}{6} = \frac{24}{3} = 8, \quad \frac{24}{6} = \frac{12}{3} = 4, \quad \frac{58}{6} = \frac{58}{6}$

58 is prime number; The answer is 58.

9) Answer: C.

$x^2 - 81 = 0 \Rightarrow x^2 = 81 \Rightarrow x = 9$

10) Answer: B.

If $a = 6$ then $b = \frac{6^2}{4} + 4 \Rightarrow b = \frac{36}{4} + 4 \Rightarrow b = 9 + 4 = 13$

Practice Tests 1

Section 2: College–Level Mathematics

1) Answer: A.

$$\frac{\sqrt{27a^5b^3}}{\sqrt{3ab^2}} = \frac{3a^2b\sqrt{3ab}}{b\sqrt{3a}} = 3a^2\sqrt{b}$$

2) Answer: D.

$\tan\left(-\frac{\pi}{4}\right) = -1$

3) Answer: C.

$$\begin{cases} 4x + y = 8 \\ 8x - 6y = -16 \end{cases} \Rightarrow \text{Multiplication (-2) in first equation} \Rightarrow$$

$$\begin{cases} -8x - 2y = -16 \\ 8x - 6y = -16 \end{cases}$$

Add two equations together $\Rightarrow -8y = -32 \Rightarrow y = 4$ then: $x = 1$

4) Answer: D.

$E = 5 + A$

$A = S - 4$

5) Answer: B.

$(x - h)^2 + (y - k)^2 = r^2 \Rightarrow$ center: (h, k) and radius: r

$(x - 4)^2 + (y + 5)^2 = 18 \Rightarrow$ center: $(4, -5)$ and radius: $3\sqrt{2}$

6) Answer: D.

$c(3) = (3)^2 + 5(3) + 30 = 9 + 15 + 30 = 54$

$6 \times 3 = 18 \Rightarrow 18 - 54 = -36 \Rightarrow 36{,}000$ loss

7) Answer: B.

$\frac{|3+x|}{7} \leq 6 \Rightarrow |3 + x| \leq 42 \Rightarrow -42 \leq 3 + x \leq 42 \Rightarrow -42 - 3 \leq x \leq 42 - 3 \Rightarrow -45 \leq x \leq 39$

8) Answer: C.

$$-5y = -4x - 12 \Rightarrow y = \frac{-4}{-5}x - \frac{12}{-5} \Rightarrow y = \frac{4}{5}x + \frac{12}{5}$$

9) Answer: D.

$$(g-f)(x) = g(x) - f(x) = (-x^2 - 1 - 3x) - (4 + x)$$
$$-x^2 - 1 - 3x - 4 - x = -x^2 - 4x - 5$$

10) Answer: B.

$$\sin B = \frac{\text{the length of the side that is opposite that angle}}{\text{the length of the longest side of the triangle}} = \frac{5}{6}$$

Answers and Explanations

TSI Mathematics

Practice Tests 2

Section 1: Arithmetic and Elementary Algebra

1) Answer: C.

$7^5 \times 7^8 = 7^{5+8} = 7^{13}$

2) Answer: B.

Simplify:

$11 + 2x \leq 15 \Rightarrow 2x \leq 15 - 11 \Rightarrow 2x \leq 4 \Rightarrow x \leq 2$

3) Answer: B.

$44 - \$32.52 = \$11.48$

4) Answer: D.

Simplify:

$$\frac{\frac{1}{2} - \frac{x+5}{4}}{\frac{x^2}{2} - \frac{5}{2}} = \frac{\frac{1}{2} - \frac{x+5}{4}}{\frac{x^2 - 5}{2}} = \frac{2(\frac{1}{2} - \frac{x+5}{4})}{x^2 - 5} \Rightarrow \text{Simplify: } \frac{1}{2} - \frac{x+5}{4} = \frac{-x-3}{4}$$

then: $\dfrac{2(\frac{-x-3}{4})}{x^2 - 5} = \dfrac{\frac{-x-3}{2}}{x^2 - 5} = \dfrac{-x-3}{2(x^2 - 5)} = \dfrac{-x-3}{2x^2 - 10}$

5) Answer: A.

$75 \times \dfrac{x}{100} = 15 \Rightarrow 75 \times x = 1500 \Rightarrow x = \dfrac{2500}{75} = 20$

6) Answer: B.

Underline the tenth place: 2364.47245

Look to the right if it is 5 or above, give it a shove.

Then, round up to 2364.5

7) Answer: C.

$\sqrt{58} = 7.615773...$

then: $\sqrt{58}$ is between 7 and 8

8) Answer: D.

$\frac{a+b}{2} = 8 \Rightarrow a + b = 16$

$\frac{a+b+c}{3} = 9 \Rightarrow a + b + c = 27$

$16 + c = 27 \Rightarrow c = 27 - 16 = 11$

9) Answer: A.

Number of squares equal to: $\frac{24 \times 18}{3 \times 3} = 8 \times 6 = 48$

10) Answer: C.

Use FOIL (First, Out, In, Last)

$(x - 4)(x^2 + 6x + 2) = x^3 + 6x^2 + 2x - 4x^2 - 24x - 8$

$= x^3 + 2x^2 - 22x - 8$

TSI Math Workbook

Practice Tests 2

Section 2: College–Level Mathematics

1) Answer: D.

$\frac{x^3}{12} \Rightarrow$ reciprocal is: $\frac{12}{x^3}$

2) Answer: A.

$\cos 60° = \frac{1}{2}$

3) Answer: C.

$\sin\theta = \frac{4}{5} \Rightarrow$ we have following triangle, then

$c = \sqrt{5^2 - 4^2} = \sqrt{25 - 16} = \sqrt{9} = 3$

$\cos\theta = \frac{3}{5}$

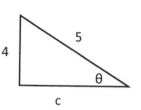

4) Answer: B.

$\begin{cases} -4x - y = -4 \\ 8x - 2y = 8 \end{cases} \Rightarrow$ Multiplication (−2) in first equation $\Rightarrow$

$\begin{cases} 8x + 2y = 8 \\ 8x - 2y = 8 \end{cases}$

Add two equations together $\Rightarrow 16x = 16 \Rightarrow x = 1$, then: $y = 0$

5) Answer: D.

METHOD ONE:

$\log_2 x = 3$

Apply logarithm rule: $a = \log_b(b^a) \Rightarrow 3 = \log_2(2^3) = \log_2(8)$

$\log_2 x = \log_2(8)$

When the logs have the same base:

$\log_b(f(x)) = \log_b(g(x)) \Rightarrow f(x) = g(x)$ then: $x = 8$

METHOD TWO:

We know that: $\log_a b = c \Rightarrow b = a^c$ $\log_2 x = 3 \Rightarrow x = 2^3 = 8$

6) Answer: D.

METHOD ONE:

$\log_4(x+3) - \log_4(x-3) = 1$

Add $\log_4(x-3)$ to both sides

$\log_4(x+3) - \log_4(x-3) + \log_4(x-3) = 1 + \log_4(x-3)$

$\log_4(x+3) = 1 + \log_4(x-3)$

Apply logarithm rule: $a = \log_b(b^a) \Rightarrow 1 = \log_4(4^1) = \log_4(4)$

then: $\log_4(x+3) = \log_4(4) + \log_4(x-3)$

Logarithm rule: $\log_c(a) + \log_c(b) = \log_c(ab)$

then: $\log_4(4) + \log_4(x-3) = \log_4(4(x-3))$

$\log_4(x+3) = \log_4(4(x-3))$

When the logs have the same base:

$\log_b(f(x)) = \log_b(g(x)) \Rightarrow f(x) = g(x)$

$(x+3) = 4(x-3) \Rightarrow x = \frac{15}{3} = 5$

METHOD TWO:

We know that: $\log_a b - \log_a c = \log_a \frac{b}{c}$ and $\log_a b = c \Rightarrow b = a^c$

Then $\log_4(x+3) - \log_4(x-3) = \log_4 \frac{x+3}{x-3} = 1 \Rightarrow \frac{x+3}{x-3} = 4^1 = 4 \Rightarrow x+3 = 4(x-3)$

$\Rightarrow x + 3 = 4x - 12 \Rightarrow 4x - x = 12 + 3 \to 3x = 15 \Rightarrow x = \frac{15}{3} = 5$

7) Answer: C.

$|9 - (12 \div |2 - 8|)| = |9 - (12 \div |-6|)| = |9 - (12 \div 6)| = |9 - 2| = |7| = 7$

8) Answer: C.

$$f(x) = x - \frac{7}{3} \Rightarrow y = x - \frac{7}{3} \Rightarrow y + \frac{7}{3} = x \Rightarrow f^{-1}(x) = x + \frac{75}{3}$$

$f^{-1}(2) = 2 + \frac{7}{3} = \frac{13}{3}$

9) Answer: C.

$f(x) = \ln(2x - 1) \Rightarrow y = \ln(2x - 1)$

Change variables x and y: $x = \ln(2y - 1)$

solve: $x = \ln(2y - 1)$

$y = \frac{e^x + 1}{2} = \frac{1}{2}(e^x + 1)$

10) Answer: B.

$e^{4x+1} = 10$

If $f(x) = g(x)$, then $\ln(f(x)) = \ln(g(x))$

$\ln(e^{4x+1}) = \ln(10)$

Apply logarithm rule: $\log_a(x^b) = b \log_a(x)$

$\ln(e^{4x+1}) = (4x + 1)\ln(e)$

$(4x + 1)\ln(e) = \ln(10)$

$(4x + 1)\ln(e) = (4x + 1)$

$(4x + 1) = \ln(10) \Rightarrow x = \frac{\ln(10) - 1}{4}$

"End"

Made in the USA
Middletown, DE
22 May 2019